EXPERIENCING THE TORAH

JOEL LURIE GRISHAVER

TORAH AURA PRODUCTIONS

ISBN 10: 1-934527-44-0

ISBN 13: 978-1-934527-44-3

Torah Aura Productions • 4423 Fruitland Avenue, Los Angeles, CA 90058
(800) BE-Torah • (800) 238-6724 • (323) 585-7312 • fax (323) 585-0327
E-MAIL <misrad@torahaura.com> • Visit the Torah Aura website at www.torahaura.com

Manufactured in the United States of America

TABLE OF CONTENTS

INTRODUCTION: EXPERIENCE!

We are taught that the real idea of studying Torah is to learn that it is not a collection of stories about other people but rather the stories of our own experiences. This book, *Experiencing the Torah,* is about turning the Torah into experiences and then finding ourselves in those events.

We start by performing the **Biblical Text** out loud. Originally, long before printing, the Torah was about hearing, not reading. These scripts let us hear the Torah and put our own spin on the emotions and feelings expressed by the biblical characters.

Next we have **Delving Deeper** sections. These let us look into specific word patterns in the Torah and find what famous commentators have said about those words. This section, too, ends in an expression of our feelings and finding our own meaning in the text.

Finally we have **Experiences**. These activities allow us to create our own understanding of the Torah. They let us fit ourselves into the text. And they let us fit the text inside us. This is the way that Jews have always studied Torah, turning its words into experiences.

THE GARDEN (GENESIS 2:4–5:25)

This is actually the second story in the Torah. First there is a general story of creation that goes day by day through the first seven days. Now we move in closer and get the story of Adam and Eve.

PART I: THE GARDEN GROWS

Narrator 1: ²⁴This is the family-history of the skies and the land and their creation from the day that Adonai, the God, made land and skies. ⁵There were not yet plants of the field in the land, there were not yet grasses of the field growing—because Adonai, the God, had not yet caused it to rain on the land—and because there was no Earthling to work the earth. ⁶A mist went up from the ground and gave drink to the whole face of the earth.

Narrator 2: [7]Adonai, the God, formed the Earthling from the dust of the earth and breathed into his nose the soul of life. The Earthling had a living spirit.

Narrator 1: [8]Adonai, the God, planted a Garden in Eden and put there the Earthling who had been shaped. [9]Adonai, the God, made trees grow from the earth, every kind of tree which is nice to look at and good to eat. The Tree of Life was in the middle of the Garden and the Tree of the Knowledge of Good from Evil... [15]Adonai, the God, took the Earthling and put him in the Garden of Eden, to work it and to keep it. [16]Then God commanded the Earthling:

God: You may eat from every other tree in the garden except from the Tree of [17]the Knowledge of Good from Evil. You may not eat from it. On the day you eat from it, your death will come.

Narrator 2: [18]Adonai, the God, said:

God: It is not good that the Earthling is alone. I will make a companion who fits with the Earthling.

Narrator 1: [19]So Adonai, the God, formed from the soil all the wild beasts and all the birds. And brought each to the Earthling to see what the Earthling would call it. [20]Whatever the Earthling called the animal, that became its name... But for the Earthling, no helper who fit could be found.

Narrator 2: [21]Adonai, the God, made the Earthling sleep a deep sleep and took one rib and then closed in the flesh. [22]Adonai, the God, built the rib into a woman, and brought her to the Earthling.

Narrator 1: [23]The Earthling said:

Adam: This is the one, bone from my bone, flesh from my flesh. She shall be called Woman because she was taken from Man.

Narrator 2: [24]So a man will leave his father and his mother, he will cling to his wife, and they will become one flesh. [25]Now the two of them, the Earthling and his wife, were naked, but they were not embarrassed.

PART II: THE GARDEN DIVIDES AND REPRODUCES

Narrator 1: ³¹The snake was the sneakiest of the animals which Adonai, the God, had made. It said to the woman:

Snake: Did God really say that you may not eat from any of the trees in the Garden?

Narrator 2: ²The woman said to the snake:

Woman: We may eat the fruit from any of the other trees in the garden, ³but God said: "The fruit from the tree in the middle of the garden, you may not eat it, and you may not touch it, or you will die."

Narrator 1: ⁴The snake said to the woman:

Snake: You are not going to die. ⁵Rather, God knows that on the day you eat from it, your eyes will be opened and you will be like gods, knowing "good" from "evil."

Narrator 2: ⁶The woman saw that the tree was good for eating, that it was nice to look at and that the tree was a source of knowledge. She took a fruit and ate it. She gave it to her husband and he ate it.

Narrator 1: **The eyes of the two of them** were opened, and they knew that they were naked. They sewed together fig leaves and made themselves clothing.

Narrator 2: ⁸They heard the sound of Adonai, the God, walking around in the garden at the windy time of the day. The Earthling and his wife hid themselves from Adonai, the God, in the middle of the trees of the Garden.

THE EYES OF THE TWO OF THEM (GENESIS 3:7)

The Torah says that after they ate the fruit of the Tree of Knowledge:

THE EYES OF THE TWO OF THEM WERE OPENED, AND THEY KNEW THAT THEY WERE NAKED. THEY SEWED TOGETHER FIG LEAVES AND MADE THEMSELVES CLOTHING.

One would have expected the Torah to say "THEIR EYES (עֵינֵיהֶם eineihem) WERE OPEN." But it actually says (עֵינֵי שְׁנֵיהֶם einei sh'neihem) "THE EYES OF THE TWO OF THEM WERE OPENED." This teaches that after they ate from the Tree of Knowledge they realized that they were two different people, separate from each other. (Rabbi Bunim)

What do you think they saw differently after they ate the fruit?

9

Narrator 1: [9]Adonai, the God, called to the Earthling and said to him:

God: Where are you?

Narrator 1: [10]He said:

Adam: I heard you in the garden and I was afraid because I was naked, so I hid.

Narrator 2: [11]God said:

God: Who told you that you were naked? Did you eat from the tree that I commanded you not to eat from?

Narrator 1: [12]The Earthling said:

Adam: The woman whom you gave me to stand with me gave me from the tree and I ate.

Narrator 2: [13]God said to the woman:

God: What have you done?

Narrator 1: She said:

Woman: The snake seduced me and I ate.

Narrator 2: [14]God said to the snake:

God: Because you have done this, you are cursed among all beasts and among all living things. You will walk on your stomach. You will eat dust all the days of your life. [15]I will make you and the woman into enemies—your future-family will be enemies with her future-family. They will beat your head and you will bite their heels.

Narrator 1: [16]To the woman God said:

God: I will increase the pain you feel. With pain you will give birth to children. Your man's closeness you shall seek, but he shall rule over you.

Narrator 2: [17]And God said to the Earthling:

God: Because you listened to your woman and ate from the tree from which I commanded you not to eat, the earth will be cursed. With hard work you shall eat from it all the days of your life. ¹⁸Thorns and thistles shall grow from the earth. **¹⁹With the sweat of your brow you shall get bread to eat until you return to the earth** from which you were taken. For you are dust and to dust you will return.

Narrator 1: ²⁰Then the Earthling called his woman by the name

Adam: Eve,

Narrator 1: which means "the giver of life", because she was going to be the mother of all the living.

Narrator 2: ²¹Adonai made Adam and Eve clothing and dressed them. ²²Adonai, the God, said:

God: Now people have become like Us, knowing Good from Evil. Next, they could take and eat from the Tree of Life and live forever.

Narrator 2: ²³So Adonai, the God, banished them from the Garden of Eden to work the earth from which they were taken. ²⁴After they were driven out God settled them to the east of Eden. God placed a flaming ever-turning sword to guard the path to the Tree of Life.

WITH THE SWEAT OF YOUR BROW YOU SHALL GET BREAD TO EAT UNTIL YOU RETURN TO THE EARTH (GENESIS 3:19)

Here the Torah says, "WITH THE SWEAT OF YOUR BROW YOU SHALL GET BREAD TO EAT UNTIL YOU RETURN TO THE EARTH (3:18)." The word שׁוּב shuv means "RETURN" and hints at תְּשׁוּבָה t'shuvah, meaning "repentance." Once you return to God by repenting, you will find pleasure in your work and purpose to your life. (Hillel Zeitlin)

Why do you think God made Adam and Eve earn their own food rather than continuing to feed them as had been done in the Garden?

Experiences

Do one of these things.

Paper-Tear Midrash

A paper-tear midrash is an artistic creation made with paper and glue. No scissors, no knives, no rulers, and no pens or pencils may be used.

Make your own paper-tear midrash of one of the following:

- What Eve saw when she first opened her eyes.
- Adam names the animals and the birds.
- The Tree in the middle of the Garden of Eden.
- Adam and Eve leaving the Garden of Eden.

Design a Tree of Life/Tree of Knowledge

Break into groups. Each group should have twelve paper leaves. On six of them they should write things that should hang on the Tree of Life. On six of them they should write things that should hang on the Tree of Knowledge. Trade leaves with another group. Try to figure out which leaves went with each tree. Decorate your room with your leaves.

Shoot a Video

Make a video midrash of one of the following:

- Adam and Eve's first conversation.
- God deciding to put the tree in the middle of the Garden.
- Eve talking Adam into eating the fruit.
- Adam and Eve leaving the Garden.

CAIN AND ABEL (GENESIS 4: 1–26)

Cain and Abel are the children of Adam and Eve.

PROLOGUE

Narrator 1: 4:1Adam knew his wife Eve. She became pregnant and gave birth to Cain. She said:

Eve: **Cain means "I got a man with God's help."**

Narrator 1: 2Later on she gave birth to Abel, his brother. Abel became a shepherd. Cain farmed the earth.

THE STORY

Narrator 2: 3When time passed, Cain brought the fruit of the earth as a gift-offering for Adonai. 4And Abel brought the best firstborn of his flock. 5Adonai accepted Abel and his gift, but Cain and his gift Adonai didn't accept.

CAIN MEANS "I GOT A MAN WITH GOD'S HELP" (GENESIS 4:1)

When Cain is born, Eve gives him a big, powerful name. When Abel is born, there is no explanation of his name. The word הֶבֶל *hevel* (Abel) usually means "bad tidings." The difference in their parents' expectations caused the fight.

(Rabbi Israel of Rizhin)

What do you think caused the jealousy?

13

Narrator 1: Cain grew angry. His face fell. ⁶Adonai said to Cain:

God: Why are you angry? Why has your face fallen? ⁷When you are good aren't you lifted up? But when you don't do good, sin haunts your door, ready to tempt you. But you can master it.

Narrator 1: ⁸Cain said something to his brother Abel. When they were in the field, Cain rose up upon his brother, Abel, and killed him.

Narrator 2: ⁹Adonai said to Cain:

God: Where is your brother Abel?

Narrator 2: He said:

Cain: I don't know. Am I my brother's keeper?

Narrator 2: ¹⁰God said:

God: What have you done? The voice of your brother's bloods shouts to Me from the earth. ¹¹From now on, you are cursed from the earth because the earth opened up its mouth to take your brother's bloods from your hand. ¹²From now on, when you work the earth it will no longer give you strength. You will be hunted and wander homeless over the land.

Narrator 1: ¹³Cain said:

Cain: My punishment is too great to bear. ¹⁴I have been banished today from the face of the earth, and from Your face I will be hidden as well. I will wander homeless over the land. Therefore, whoever meets me may kill me.

Narrator 1: ¹⁵Adonai said,

God: Whoever kills Cain…will be punished.

Narrator 1: Adonai put a mark on Cain so whoever met him would know not to kill him. ¹⁶Cain went from before God's face. He settled in the land of Nod (which means "wandering"), east of Eden.

EPILOGUE

Narrator 1: [17]Cain knew his woman. She got pregnant and gave birth to a son, Enoch. Cain built a town and called the name of the town like the name of his son,

Cain: Enoch.

Narrator 2: [18]Enoch fathered Irad. Irad fathered Mehuyael. Mehuyael fathered Metusael. Metusael fathered Lamekh. [19]Lamekh took two women. The first was named Adah. The second was named Tzillah. [20]Adah birthed Yaval. He was the father of those who live in tents with livestock. [21]His brother's name was Yuval. He was the father of all who play the lyre and the pipe. [22] And Tzillah also birthed Tuval-Cain, the one who forged bronze and iron tools, and Tuval-Cain's sister, Na'amah.

Narrator 1: [23]Lamekh said to his women,

Lamekh: Adah and Tzillah, listen to me.
Women of Lamekh, give ear to my voice.
I have killed a man for wounding me,
a child for bruising me. [24]Cain is to be avenged only seven times, while Lamekh will be avenged seventy-seven times.

Narrator 2: [25]Adam knew his woman again. She birthed a son. She called his name:

Eve: Seth.

Narrator 1: God has put another seed in Abel's place because Cain had killed him.

Narrator 2: [26]A son was born to Seth also. He called his name Enosh. Then they began to call upon the name of Adonai.

THIS IS THE BOOK OF THE GENERATIONS OF ADAM

The verse after this story says:

THIS IS THE BOOK OF THE GENERATIONS OF ADAM. WHEN GOD CREATED PEOPLE, GOD MADE PEOPLE IN THE IMAGE OF GOD (Genesis 5:1).

There was a debate between Rabbi Akiva and Ben Azzai. Rabbi Akiva quoted the second half of this verse and said: "GOD MADE PEOPLE IN THE IMAGE OF GOD" is the most important idea in the Torah. Ben Azzai also quoted the first half of this verse and said, "THIS IS THE BOOK OF THE GENERATIONS OF ADAM" is more important. It makes everyone into brothers and sisters. (Jerusalem Talmud, *Nedarim* 9:9)

Have your own debate about these two phrases.

Experiences

Do one of these things.

Postcards

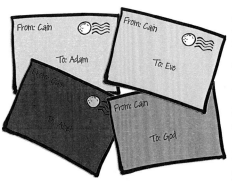

Take 5" x 7" cards and turn them into postcards. Imagine that the whole story is over. You are Cain. Address and write postcards to: (a) Adam, (b) Eve, (c) the spirit of Abel and (d) God.

Share your postcards with a group. Then pass the cards to another group. Take the cards passed to your group and write responses on the back sides.

Interviews

Rehearse with one or two partners and then perform these interviews. Add follow-up questions of your own.

- Ask Adam and Eve: Why did your sons wind up with two different jobs rather than working together?
- Ask Cain and Abel: What did you two say to each other in the field?
- Ask God: Why did you accept Abel's offering and reject Cain's? Didn't you know what would happen?
- Ask Seth: What was it like to be the next son of Adam and Eve?

Trial of Cain

Put Cain on trial for murder. In the midrash Cain argues (a) that God let Abel die, and (b) that no one had ever died before, so he had no way of knowing what would happen to Abel (*Genesis Rabbah* 22:12). Stage a trial. Decide if Cain's arguments hold up.

THE FLOOD (GENESIS 6:5–9:26)

The Flood is the story of Noah. Noah comes ten generations after Adam.

AND INTRODUCING NOAH

Narrator 1: ⁶˙⁵Adonai saw that people did a lot of evil on the land. All the urges of their hearts' thoughts were evil all day long. ⁶Adonai was uncomfortable about having made people. God's heart was pained. Adonai said:

God: ⁷I will wipe people—whom I have created—off the face of the earth. People and beasts and crawling things and sky birds—I'm uncomfortable that I made them.

Narrator 1: ⁸But Noah (meaning "comfort") found favor in Adonai's eyes.

Narrator 2: This is the family history of Noah. **Noah was a righteous person, wholesome for his generation.** Noah walked with God. [10]Noah fathered three sons: Shem, Ham, and Yafet.

[11]The land was being destroyed before God. The land was filled with violence. [12]God saw the land:

God: *Hinnei.* It has been destroyed, because each living thing has destroyed its way of living on the earth.

Narrator 2: [13]God said to Noah:

God: Before My face the end of all flesh is unavoidable, because the land is filled with violence before them. *Hinnei.* I am ready to destroy the land.

[14]Make yourself a wooden ark. Make it with rooms and cover it inside and out with tar. [15]This is how you will make it:

300 cubits long, 50 cubits wide, 30 cubits high. [16]Make an opening for light one cubit below the top. Make an opening in the ark's side. Make it with a bottom deck, a second deck, and a third deck.

Hinnei. I am bringing a flood of water on the land to destroy all flesh under the skies with breath of life in it. Everything on earth shall pass away. [18]But I will set up My covenant with you. You shall come into the ark, you, your sons, your wife and your sons' wives with you. [19]Of all that lives, of all flesh, you shall bring two of each into the ark to keep them alive with you. Let them be male and female. [20]Two of each shall come to you to keep them alive.

Narrator 1: ²²Noa<u>h</u> did all that God commanded him. He did it.

THE WATERS RISE

Narrator 2: ¹¹Adonai said to Noa<u>h</u>:

God: Come, you and all your household, into the ark. For I have seen that you are the righteous one before Me in this generation.

²Take with you seven pairs of every clean animal—a male and his female. And from every non-clean animal take two—a male and his female. ³Also, from every sky bird, take with you seven pairs of every clean animal—a male and his female—to keep species alive on the face of all the land.

⁴Because seven days from now I will make it rain upon the land for forty days and forty nights. I will wipe all established things that I have made off the face of the earth.

Narrator 1: ⁵And Noa<u>h</u> did all that Adonai commanded.

Narrator 2: ⁶Noa<u>h</u> was 600 years old when the flood came and water was upon the land.

Narrator 1: ⁷Noa<u>h</u> and his sons, and his wife, and his sons' wives came into the ark away from the face of the flood.

Narrator 2: ⁸Of every clean animal, of every animal which is not clean, of birds, and of each thing that creeps on the ground—⁹two by two they came to Noa<u>h</u>, to the ark. They came male and female, just as God commanded him.

Narrator 1: ¹⁰Seven days later the waters of the flood were over all the earth.

Narrator 2: ¹¹All the waters came up from the springs of the deepest places. The floodgates of the sky broke open.

19

Narrator 1: [12]The rain fell on the land for forty days and forty nights.

Narrator 2: [13]On that day Noa<u>h</u> and Shem, Ham, and Yafet, the sons of Noa<u>h</u> and Noa<u>h</u>'s wife, and his sons' three wives with them came into the ark. [14]Into the ark, two by two, came all living things that had the breath of life— [16]just as God had commanded.

Narrator 1: Then Adonai closed him in.

[17]The flood was on the face of the land for forty days. The waters grew and lifted the ark from on the land. [18]The waters swelled and grew very much on the land. The ark floated on the face of the waters. [19]The waters swelled and increased over the earth. All the high mountains that were under all the skies were covered.

Narrator 2: [21]Death came to all life—those that crawled on the land, the birds, the cattle, the wild animals, the swarming things that swarmed on the land—and all people.

Narrator 1: [22]Everything that had the breath of life in it, that was on dry land, died.

Narrator 2: [24]The waters swelled for 150 days.

THE WATERS RECEDE

Narrator 2: [8:1]God remembered Noa<u>h</u> and all the living things and all the animals that were with him in the ark. God brought a breath of wind across the land and the waters went down. [2]The springs of the deepest places and the floodgates of the sky were closed.

Narrator 1: The rain from the sky stopped. [3]The waters returned from covering the land. They were constantly moving and returning.

Narrator 2: After 150 days there was less water. The ark
came to rest on the mountains of Ararat. The water
kept moving and receding until the tops of the
mountains could be seen.

Narrator 1: ⁶After forty days Noah opened the window in the ark
which he had made. ⁷He sent out a raven.

Narrator 2: The raven kept leaving and returning until the
waters dried from off of the land.

Narrator 1: ⁸Then he sent out a dove to see if there was still water
on the face of the earth. ⁹But the dove could not find
a place to rest her feet, so she returned to him. (The
waters were still on the face of the earth.) He stuck
out his hand and took her and brought her to him
into the ark. ¹⁰He waited another seven days and again
sent the dove from the ark.

¹¹The dove came to him in the evening. In her beak
there were fresh olive leaves. This is how Noah knew
that the waters had gone down from on the land.
¹²He waited another seven days further, and then he
sent out the dove, but she returned to him no more.
¹³When Noah took the covering off of the ark, he saw
that the face of the earth was firm.

Narrator 2: ¹⁴The land was dry. God spoke to Noah:

God: ¹⁵Go out of the ark. You and your wife and your sons
and your son's wives with you. Bring living things that
are with you—all life: birds, animals and all crawling
things, that they can be fruitful and become many on
the earth.

Narrator 2: ¹⁶So Noah and his sons, and his wife and his
sons' wives went out of the ark. ¹⁷All living things
came out of the ark by families.

Narrator 1: [20]Noah built an altar to Adonai. He took from every clean animal and from every clean bird and burnt offerings on the altar. [21]Adonai smelled the comforting smell and it was said in Adonai's heart:

God: I will never again curse the soil because of people, because the urges of their hearts are evil from their youth. I will never again wipe out all living things. [22]Never again in all the earth's days will seeding time and harvest time, cold and heat, summer and winter, day and night come to an end.

Narrator 2: [9:1]God blessed Noah and his sons, saying:

God: Be fruitful and become many, and fill the land. [2]All life on the earth, every bird of the sky, all that creeps on the soil, every fish of the sea shall fear you and be terrified of you, because I put them into your hands. [3]Just like the green plants, I now give you all moving life to eat. [4]But you must not eat the flesh together with the soul-blood. [5]As for your soul-blood, I will seek responsibility from every person for the life of his or her brother or sister. [6]Whoever sheds the blood of a person by a person shall his blood be shed, because God created people in God's image.

[7]Be fruitful and become many, and fill the earth, and become many on it.

THE COVENANT

Narrator 2: [8]God said to Noah and to his sons with him:

God: [9]*Hineni*, I now establish my covenant with you and with your future-family after you and with every living thing that was with you…that went off the ark—with all life on the land. I will establish my covenant with you. Never again will all life be wiped out by the waters of a flood. Never again will there be a flood to destroy the land.

Narrator 2: [17]Then God said:

God: This is a sign of the covenant that I give between Me and you, and with all the living things with you for all generations to come. [13]I give my rainbow in the clouds, which will be the sign of the covenant between Me and the land. [14]Whenever I fill the skies with clouds—whenever a rainbow appears in those clouds—[15]I will remember My covenant. Never again will waters become a flood to destroy all life.

[16]When the rainbow is in the clouds I will look at it and remember my everlasting covenant.

Narrator 2: [17]God said to Noa<u>h</u>:

God: That is the sign of the covenant which I established between Me and between all life which is on the land.

WHEN THE RAINBOW IS IN THE CLOUDS I WILL LOOK AT IT AND REMEMBER MY EVERLASTING COVENANT (GENESIS 9:16).

How does the rainbow symbolize peace, unity and the continued existence of the world? It is because the rainbow is composed of a number of colors, shades and hues, and all of this unified into a single whole. The same is true with the differences between people, groups, and nations. A life based on mutual understanding and tolerance, on harmony and peace, is the basis for the existence of the world. (Z. Hillel)

What does the rainbow mean to you?

Experiences

Do one of these things.

Environmental Education

Design an ark. Make a 2-D or 3-D model to show all the things that will be needed to care for all the animals. First make a list of things that every animal needs. Then try to meet the needs of all the living beings on the ark.

Noah's Farewell to the Troops

Imagine that the time on the ark is over. It is time to say good-bye to all those who are on the ark and spread out and cover the earth. Work as a speech writing team and create a wonderful final address for Noah.

Covenantal Congress

Write a covenant with God. Create a list of things we should promise God that we will do (and not do). Finish your document and have everyone in the class sign it.

ABRAM AND SARAI COME TO CANAAN (GENESIS 10:1, 11:10–12:9)

To get from the flood to Abram and Sarai we build the Tower of Babel, spread out, and go another ten generations.

THE BACK STORY

Narrator 1: ¹⁰:¹Noah fathered three sons: Shem, Ham and Yafet. They in turn fathered sons after the flood.

Narrator 2: ¹¹:¹⁰This is the family history of Shem. Shem was one hundred years old when he fathered Arpachshad two years after the flood.

Narrator 1: ¹²Arpachshad fathered Shela_h_.

Narrator 2: ¹⁴Shela_h_ fathered Eber.

Narrator 1: ¹⁶Eber fathered Peleg.

Narrator 2: [18]Peleg fathered Reu.

Narrator 1: [20]Reu fathered Serug.

Narrator 2: [22]Serug fathered Nahor.

Narrator 1: [24]Nahor fathered Terah. [26]When Terah was seventy years old he fathered Abram, Nahor and Haran.

Narrator 2: [27]This is the family history of Terah.

Terah fathered Abram, Nahor and Haran. Haran fathered Lot. [28]Haran died before his father, in the land of his birth, Ur Kasdim. [29]Both Abram and Nahor married. Abram's wife was named Sarai. The name of Nahor's wife was Milcah, who was the daughter of Haran, who was the father of Milcah and Iscah. [30]Sarai was barren, she had no child.

Narrator 1: [31]Terah took Abram, his son, and Lot, son of Haran, his grandson, and Sarai, his daughter-in-law, Abram's wife. Together they left Ur Kasdim to go to the land of Canaan. They went as far as Haran and settled there. [32]Terah lived 205 years. Terah died in Haran (long after his son Abram had left).

THE MOMENT

Narrator 2: [12:1]Adonai said to Abram:

God: **Take yourself** from your land, from your birthplace, from your father's house, to the land: There I will let you see.

TAKE YOURSELF (GENESIS 12:1)

Every Jew must "travel toward himself or herself,—to his roots— because that is the Jews' purpose. (Rabbi Aharon of Karlin)

How is the purpose of a Jew to "travel toward" himself or herself?

²And I will make you a great nation. And I will bless you. And I will make your name great. And you will be a blessing. **³And I will bless those who bless you.** And I will curse anyone who curses you. All the families of the earth will be blessed through you.

Narrator 2: ⁴Abram went as Adonai had told him. And Lot went with him. Abram was seventy-five years old when he left Haran. ⁵Abram took Sarai his wife and Lot his nephew, and all they owned, and all their people who they gathered in Haran, and they left to go to the land of Canaan.

Narrator 1: They came to the land of Canaan. ⁶Abram crossed the land to the place of Shechem, to the Oak of Moreh. The Canaanites were then living in the land. ⁷Adonai was seen by Abram and said:

God: To your future-family I will give this land.

Narrator 1: And he built an altar there, to Adonai, Who had been seen by him. ⁸From there he moved on to the hills east of Beth El. He spread his tent with Beth El seaward and Ai toward sunrise. He built an altar there to Adonai. He called on the name of Adonai. ⁹Abram traveled stage by stage southward, toward the Negev.

AND I WILL BLESS THOSE WHO BLESS YOU (GENESIS 12:3)

The verse continues: AND I WILL CURSE ANYONE WHO CURSES YOU (Genesis 12:3).

A person should try hard to have a lot of people who like him and a few that dislike him. That is the only way the world can exist in harmony. That which you do to get people to like you will cause some people to dislike you. (Ralbag)

Why do you have to expect some people to dislike you?

Experiences

Do one of these things.

Interviews

Imagine that you are a reporter. Conduct the following interviews.

- Say to Abram: "In the Torah, nothing is said about (a) your journey to Canaan or (b) your entry into the land. Tell us what happened."
- Do the same with Sarai.
- Do the same with Lot.
- Ask God: "What made you decide that you wanted to give one family a lot of extra attention, and what made you think that Sarai and Abram's family should be that family?"

Map the Journey

Research on the Internet. Find the path of Abram's journeys. Make your own map.

Diary Entries

Write a diary entry in the diary of Abram, Sarai, or Lot for the day they left home and headed toward the land of Canaan.

ABRAM BECOMES ABRAHAM (GENESIS 17:1–23)

In our last story Abram, Lot, and Sarai came to Canaan. In Canaan they have a series of experiences. There is a famine that causes the family to move to Egypt. Abram and Lot split up. Abram fights in the War of the Kings and rescues Lot. Then there is a covenant between cut pieces. Ishmael is born, with Hagar serving as a surrogate for Sarai. Now, with this story, things begin to change.

Narrator 1: ¹When Abram was ninety-nine years old, Adonai appeared to Abram and said to him:

WALK BEFORE ME AND BE THE BEST (GENESIS 17:1)

The Hebrew word תָּמִים *tamim*, which we translate as "the best", can also be "pure" or "simple". Here it is used to say "be circumcised" because this is the passage in which God demands circumcision. The text was a hard one for Abraham, not only because he was old, but because it would make it much harder to convince other people to become Jewish. Bringing people to God was important to Sarah and Abraham. (*Orhot Tzaddikim*)

Why do you think God makes circumcision a mitzvah?

God: I am God, Shaddai. **Walk before me and be the best.** ²I put my covenant between Me and you. I will make you very, very many.

Narrator 2: ³Abram bowed to the ground. God spoke with him:

God: ⁴As for me, here is my covenant with you—you will become the father of many nations. ⁵No longer will your name be called Abram. Instead your name will be Abraham, for I will make you *Av Hamon Goyyim* (the father of many nations). ⁶Many nations and rulers will come from you.

⁷I set up My covenant between Me and between you and your future-family after you. It is an everlasting covenant. I will be God to you and to your future-family. ⁸I will give to you and to your future-family the land where you are staying. All the land of Canaan will be yours forever.

Narrator 1: ⁹God said to Abraham:

God: As for you, you are to keep my covenant, you and your future-family. ¹⁰This is my covenant. Circumcise every male. That will be the sign of the covenant between Me and between you. ¹¹When eight days old, every boy should be circumcised.

Narrator 2: ¹⁵God said to Abraham:

God: As for Sarai your wife, don't call her Sarai anymore, because Sarah (meaning "princess") is now her name. ¹⁶I will bless her and I will give you a son from her. I will bless her, and nations and rulers will come from her.

Narrator 1: [17]Abraham fell to the ground laughing. He thought:

Abraham: How is a hundred-year-old man going to father a son? How is ninety-year-old Sarah going to give birth?

Narrator 2: [18]Abraham said to God:

Abraham: If only Ishmael would live before you.

God: [19]Sarah, your wife, will yet give birth to a son. **You will name him Isaac (meaning "he laughs")**. I will set up my covenant with him as an everlasting covenant.

[20]As for Ishmael, I hear you. I bless him. I will make him fruitful. I will make him very, very many. He will father twelve princes. I will make a great nation of him.

[21]But My covenant I will set up with Isaac.

Narrator: [22]When God finished speaking with him, God went up from Abraham. [23]Abraham took Ishmael, his son, and all the males among Abraham's household, and circumcised them. Abraham was ninety-nine years old when he was circumcised. Ishmael was thirteen years old when he was circumcised. On that very day Abraham, Ishmael his son, and all of his household were circumcised.

YOU WILL NAME HIM ISAAC (MEANING "HE LAUGHS")
(GENESIS 17:9)

Humans named Abram, Sarai, and Jacob. God then changed their names and changed the direction of their lives. God named Isaac and never changed his name. (Jerusalem Talmud, Brakhot 1:6)

What is the lesson that can be learned here?

Experiences

Do one of these things.

Sarah's Nameplate

Design a sign, plaque or nameplate for Sarah to celebrate her new name. Write a narrative describing the meaning of each of the symbols you use.

Sarah Video

The biblical text is a dialogue between God and Abraham. Now create and shoot a video of God talking to Sarah. Remember to keep God off-camera.

Role Play

- Be Abraham and tell everyone about your conversation with God. Share all the news God gave you in this talk.
- Be Sarah: How do you feel about all the decisions that God has made for your life and told to your husband?
- Be Ishmael: How do you feel about your father and his God? What about the demands now made on your life?
- Be Hagar: How did you feel about your son's circumcision?

Brit Milah Event

Invite a doctor, a mohel, a mohellet, or a rabbi to come into your class and explain *brit milah* (circumcision).

SARAH LAUGHED (GENESIS 18:1–12)

This story happens directly after the name-change story.

THE VISITORS

Narrator 1: ^{18:1}**Now Adonai appeared to him by the Oaks of Mamre.** He was sitting at the entrance of the tent during the heat of the day. ²He lifted his eyes and saw and *hinnei* suddenly three men were standing over him. He saw them and ran toward them. He bowed to the ground and said:

NOW ADONAI APPEARED TO HIM IN THE OAKS OF MAMRE
(GENESIS 18:1)

The Torah says "to him" and not "to Abraham." Each of us can be that "him." God appears to each of us in our "Oaks of Mamre." Oaks of Mamre is אֵלֹנֵי מַמְרֵא *Elonei Mamre*. *Elonei* means "strong." Mamre has to do with rebellion. Even if a person is rebellious, God still appears to him or her. (*Me'or Einayim*)

Has God appeared to you yet? Do you have a "place of rebellion"?

Abraham: ³My masters, please, if I have found favor in your eyes, please do not pass by me. ⁴Please let me bring you a little water. Wash your feet and rest under the tree. ⁵Let me bring you some bread.

Visitors: Do just what you have said.

Narrator 2: ⁶Abraham hurried into Sarah's tent.

Abraham: Hurry, three measures of good flour. Knead it and bake bread.

Narrator 1: ⁷Abraham ran to the herd. He took a tender calf and gave it to a servant, so that he could hurry to prepare it. ⁸He took yogurt and milk and the calf that had been cooked, and served it to them. He stood by them under the tree while they ate.

THE ANNOUNCEMENT

Visitors: ⁹Where is Sarah, your wife?

Abraham: Right here in the tent.

Voice 1: ¹⁰I will definitely return at the time of birth, when Sarah your wife will have a son.

SARAH LAUGHS

Narrator 2: Sarah was listening at the entrance to the tent. ¹¹Abraham and Sarah were old. Sarah was too old to have a child. ¹²Sarah laughed and said to herself:

Sarah: Now that my time has passed, **how can my old husband and I have a child**?

HOW CAN MY OLD HUSBAND AND I HAVE A CHILD?
(GENESIS 18:12-13)

Sarah laughs and says, "Now that my time has passed, how can my old husband and I have a child?" (Genesis 18:12)

God reports Sarah's words to Abraham, saying, "Will I really give birth, now that I am old?" (Genesis 18:13).

How do the words change? Why did you think God did the edit?

Narrator 1: [13]Adonai said to Abraham:

God: Why is Sarah laughing and saying, "Will I really give birth, now that I am old?" [14]Is any miracle too great for Adonai? I will return to you at the time of birth, when Sarah will have a son.

Sarah: [15]I did not laugh.

Narrator 2: She was afraid. She was answered:

Voice 2: You did so laugh.

Narrator 1: [16]The men got up from there and looked down on Sodom. Abraham walked along with them.

Experiences

Do one of these things.

Voice 1, Voice 2

The lines given to "Voice 1" and "Voice 2" are mysteries. Some people think that they are said by God. Others think that they are just the visitors speaking. Likewise, some people believe that the guests are angels. Others think that they are people with a message. Decide who is speaking in these two cases.

Write a Guide to Hospitality

Write "Abraham and Sarah's Guide to Welcoming Strangers."

Laugh Track

Have each member of the class record an interpretation of Sarah's laugh and the line she said afterward: "Now that my time has passed, how can my old husband and I have a child?"

THE SODOM DEBATE (GENESIS 18:17–33)

This story, too, follows directly.

TO DO WHAT IS RIGHT AND JUST
(GENESIS 18.19)

The word for charity is צְדָקָה *tzedakah*. It means not just charity but righteousness. Once it had mentioned doing what is "right," why did the Torah have to add "just"? Isn't right automatically just?

One could think that in order to raise charity one could mess around with ethics a little. After all, if the money is going to do good, can we cheat a little bit to raise more? God's answer is no. It takes both doing the right thing and doing it in a just way. *(Yalkut ha-Gershum)*

When does the end justify the means?

GOD'S MONOLOGUE

Narrator 1: ¹⁸˙¹⁷Adonai said:

God: Should I hide what I am going to do from Abraham, ¹⁸since Abraham is to become a great and numerous nation, and all the nations of the world will be blessed through him? ¹⁹I have become close to him so that he will command his children and his future-family to keep the way of Adonai, **to do what is right and just.**

Narrator 2: ²⁰Adonai said to Abraham:

God: The shouting from Sodom and Gomorrah is very loud. And their sin is very heavy. [21]I will go down and I will see if they are really doing as they are shouting.

THE DEBATE

Narrator 1: [22]The men turned from there and went toward Sodom, while Abraham stayed with Adonai. [23]Abraham came close and said:

Abraham: Will you really sweep away the righteous people with the guilty ones? [24]Maybe there are fifty righteous people in the city. Will you still sweep it away? Won't you put up with the city if there are fifty righteous people there? [25]You above all should not do this thing, killing the righteous with the wicked, as if the righteous and the wicked are the same.

Should not the Judge of all the earth do what is just?

God: [26]If I find fifty righteous people inside the city, I will put up with the city.

Abraham: [27]Please...I dare to speak to my Master— even though I am only dust and ashes. [28]What if there are five less than the fifty righteous people?

Will you destroy the whole city because of five?

God: I will not destroy it if I find forty-five there.

Narrator 2: But he continued:

Abraham: Maybe only forty will be found.

God: I will not do it, because of the forty.

Abraham: [30]Please don't be angry, my Master, if I continue. Maybe only thirty will be found there.

God: I will not do it if I find thirty there.

Abraham: [31]Please, I dare speak to Adonai, maybe only twenty will be found there.

God: I will not destroy it because of the twenty.

Abraham: [32]Please don't be angry, my Master, if I continue one more time. Maybe only ten will be found there.

God: **I will not destroy it, because of the ten.**

Narrator 1: [33]Adonai left after speaking with Abraham. Abraham returned to his place.

DELVING DEEPER

I WILL NOT DESTROY IT, BECAUSE OF THE TEN
(GENESIS 18:32)

Abraham argues God down from fifty righteous people to ten. Why did he stop at ten?

A midrash teaches that there were eight righteous people on the ark: Noah and Na'amah, Shem, Ham, and Yafet and their wives. If eight good people weren't enough to stop the flood, Abraham was happy to stop at ten.

Why do you think Abraham stopped his arguing at 10?

Experiences

Do one of these things.

Interviews

Rehearse and perform one of these interviews:

1. Ask God: "Why did you tell Abraham about your plans?"
2. Ask Abraham: "How do you think you did in your argument with God? Did you win?"
3. Ask Sarah: "How do you feel about your husband arguing with God and telling God what to do?"

Write Your Own Midrash

Nineveh was also a wicked city. God sends Jonah, the prophet, to Nineveh to tell the people that they have to change. Jonah eventually does his job, and the people of Nineveh listen to him, take his words to heart, and repent. Write a midrash about a prophet that God sends to Sodom to tell the people there that they have to change their behavior.

Abraham in Darfur

Imagine Abraham arguing for human rights and dignity today. Pick a place in the world where destruction is taking place. Imagine Abraham speaking up for those people. Write his speech.

ISAAC IS BORN, HAGAR AND ISHMAEL ARE SENT AWAY
(GENESIS 21:1–21, 25:7)

After God warns Abraham that Sodom will be destroyed, Sodom is destroyed. Lot and his family escape. Abraham and family visit Abimelekh. Then this story starts with the birth of Isaac.

SARAH GIVES BIRTH

Narrator 1: ²¹˸¹Adonai remembered Sarah as Adonai had said. Adonai did for Sarah as Adonai had spoken. ²Sarah became pregnant and gave birth to a son. ³Abraham named his son Isaac (meaning "he laughs"). ⁴Abraham circumcised Isaac his son on the eighth day as God had commanded. ⁵Abraham was a son of one hundred years when Isaac his son was born to him.

Narrator 2: ⁶Sarah said:

Sarah: God has made laughter for me. Everyone who hears will laugh with me. ⁷Who would have told Abraham that Sarah would nurse sons? Well, I have given birth to a son for his old age.

Narrator 1: ⁸The boy grew, and Abraham gave a party on the day that Isaac began eating solid food.

THE ISHMAEL PROBLEM

Narrator 2: [9]But Sarah saw Ishmael, the son of Hagar the Egyptian, whom Hagar had borne to Abraham, mocking her son Isaac. [10]So she said to Abraham:

Sarah: **Throw out this slave woman with her son**, for the son of this slave woman should not inherit with my son Isaac.

Narrator 1: [11]This thing about his son (Ishmael) bothered Abraham. [12]But God said to Abraham:

God: Don't let this thing be evil in your eyes because of the boy and because of your slave woman. Whatever Sarah says to you, do as she tells you, for through Isaac shall your future-family be named. [13]But I will make a nation out of the son of the slave woman as well, because he comes from you.

THE EXILE

Narrator 2: [14]Abraham got up early in the morning. He took bread and a skin filled with water and gave it to Hagar. He put it on her shoulder and sent her away along with the child. [15]She left and wandered in the wilderness of Be'er Sheva. [16]When the water in the skin was gone, she abandoned the boy under one of the bushes. [17]Then she went and sat down across from him—a good way off—about the distance of a bowshot. She said:

Hagar: Don't let me look on the death of the child.

Narrator 2: She sat across from him. The child lifted up his voice and cried.

Narrator 1: ¹⁷God heard the voice of the lad. The angel of God called to Hagar from heaven and said to her:

Angel: What is bothering you, Hagar? Don't be afraid, because **God has heard the voice of the lad** from where he is. ¹⁸Get up, lift up the lad, and hold him tight with your hand. Because I will make him a great nation.

Narrator 1: ¹⁹Then God opened Hagar's eyes. She saw a well of water. She went and filled the skin with water and gave the lad a drink. ²⁰God was with the lad. He grew up. He lived in the wilderness and became an expert with the bow. ²¹He lived in the wilderness of Paran, and his mother took a wife for him from the land of Egypt.

CODA

Narrator 2: And much later in the Torah we find....

Narrator 1: ²⁵:⁷These are the days of the years of Abraham's life—a hundred and seventy-five years. ⁸Abraham breathed his last and died in a good old age, an old man and full of years. He was gathered to his people. ⁹Isaac and Ishmael his sons buried him in the cave of Machpelah, in the field of Ephron, the son of Zohar the Hittite, east of Mamre, ¹⁰the field that Abraham had bought from the Hittites. There Abraham was buried with Sarah his wife. ¹¹After the death of Abraham God blessed Isaac, his son. Isaac lived at Beer-la-<u>h</u>ai-roi.

GOD HEARD THE VOICE OF THE LAD (GENESIS 21:18)

The Torah doesn't record Ishmael's words. It is suggested that this was a wordless, voiceless cry—crying on the inside. God still heard his voice. Sometimes one can cry without saying a syllable. Still God hears it. (Rabbi Mendl of Worka)

When have you cried without a sound, without a syllable?

Experiences

Do one of these things.

Write the Song

Write the song that Hagar sang to Ishmael as they wandered in the wilderness.

Make a Video of the Conversation

Make a video of the conversation that happens after Sarah gets angry at Ishmael and wants him away from Isaac. Write and record the conversation between Hagar and Ishmael.

After this story is over, Isaac and Ishmael meet again at the burial of their father Abraham. Record that encounter.

Write Your Own Midrash

Write a letter from Hagar to her father, the Pharaoh of Egypt. Have her tell what happened to her and Ishmael after they left Abraham's camp. Start your story after the angel appears.

REBEKKAH AT THE WELL (GENESIS 24:1–27)

Meeting Rebekkah at the well follows two traumatic experiences. First Abraham almost sacrifices his son Isaac. Then Sarah dies and is buried in the Cave of Machpelah.

THE SETUP

Narrator 1: ^{24:1}Abraham was old, well along in days. Adonai had blessed Abraham in all things. ²Abraham said to his servant, the oldest of his house, the one in charge of all that he had:

Abraham: Please put your hand under my thigh. ³Swear by Adonai, the God of heaven and of earth, that you will not take a wife for my son from the daughters of the Canaanites with whom I live. ⁴Instead, go to my country and to my family and take a wife for my son Isaac.

Narrator 2: The servant said to him:

Servant: Maybe the woman will not be willing to follow me to this land; should I then take your son back to the land from which you came?

Abraham: ⁶Do not take my son back there. ⁷Adonai, the God of heaven, who took me from my father's house and from the land of my birth, and who spoke to me and promised me, saying:

God: To your future-family I will give this land.

Abraham: That God will send his angel before you, and you will take a wife for my son from there. ⁸But if the woman is not willing to follow you, then you will be free from this oath. No matter what, you must not take my son back there.

Narrator 1: ⁹The servant put his hand under the thigh of Abraham his master and swore to him.

REBEKKAH AT THE WELL

Narrator 2: ¹⁰The servant took ten camels and some of his master's most precious things. He got up and went to the land of Aram between the two rivers, to the city of Nahor. ¹¹He made the camels kneel down outside the city by the water well. It was evening, the time when people go out to draw water. ¹²He said:

Servant: Adonai, God of my master Abraham, please, may this be the day that you do the right thing for my master Abraham.

¹³I am standing here by the well, and the young women are going out to draw water. ¹⁴Let it be that when I say to a woman, "Please, may I drink from your jar?" one will answer:

Ideal Woman: Drink, and I will also draw water for your camels.

Servant: She will be the one that you have chosen for Isaac. And through this I will know that You have done the right thing for my master.

Narrator 2: [15]Almost before he could finish speaking there came Rebekkah, Abraham's niece. Her jar was on her shoulder. [16]She was very beautiful to look at and had never been with a man. She went down to the well, filled her jar and came up. [17]**The servant ran to meet her**.

Servant: Please, let me drink a little water from your jar.

Rebekkah: [18]Drink, my master.

Narrator 1: She hurried. She lowered her jar on her arm and let him drink. [19]When he had finished drinking, she said:

Rebekkah: I will also draw water for your camels until they have finished drinking.

Narrator 2: [20]Hurrying, she emptied her jar into the drinking trough. Again she ran to the well to draw water. She brought enough water for all the camels.

Narrator: [26]The man bowed his head and worshiped Adonai and said,

Servant: [27]Blessed be Adonai, the God of my master Abraham, who has not forsaken steadfast love and faithfulness toward my master. As for me, Adonai has led me to the house of my master's family.

THE SERVANT RAN TOWARD HER (GENESIS 24:17)

The reason that the servant ran toward her was that when she showed up, the waters of the well overflowed to meet her, and he had to get out of the way. (Rashi)

Having seen this miracle, the servant still felt the need to go on with the test. Why? Because miracles are one thing, but good deeds are a better sign. He wanted to give Rebekkah a chance to do a good deed. (Rabbi Ye<u>h</u>ezkel of Kuzmir)

What is the best thing you saw anybody ever do?

Experiences

Do one of these things.

Facebook Page

Design a Facebook page for Rebekkah.

Name: Rebekkah
Favorite activity: Being nice
Favorite hangout: The well

Interviews

Rehearse and conduct the following interviews.

- Ask Abraham: "What kind of wife do you want for Isaac?"
- Ask the servant: "How do you like the job of having to pick the right bride for Isaac? Will it be easy or hard?"
- Ask Rebekkah: "How do you feel about leaving home and moving for a husband you have not met?"

Pantomine

Rebekkah and Isaac meet in the next part of the Torah text (Genesis 24:61–67). Create a pantomime of Rebekkah meeting Isaac. Start with each of them thinking about the other before they meet. Show their feelings throughout.

JACOB: ROUND 1—BIRTH, ROUND 2—BIRTHRIGHT, ROUND 3—THE BLESSING (GENESIS 25:19–54, 27:1–40)

Before this story begins, Abraham dies and is buried by his sons.

ROUND 1: THE BIRTH

Narrator 1: [25:19]This is the family history of Isaac, son of Abraham. Abraham fathered Isaac. [20]When Isaac was forty years old he took Rebekkah as his wife. [21]Isaac pleaded with Adonai for his wife because she had not given birth to children.

Narrator 1:	Adonai allowed Isaac's plea to work, and Rebekkah became pregnant. [22]**Twins struggled in her womb**, and she said:
Rebekkah:	If it is like this, why am I living?
Narrator 2:	She went to seek out Adonai. [23]Adonai said:
God:	Two nations are in you. The two families inside you will be separated. One nation shall be stronger than the other. The older will serve the younger.
Narrator 1:	[24]When it was her time to give birth, twins were in her womb. [25]The first came out red. He was hairy like an animal skin, so they called him:
Rebekkah & Isaac:	Esau
Narrator 2:	Meaning "the hairy one". [26]After this his brother came out, his hand holding tightly to Esau's heel. They called him:
Isaac & Rebekkah:	Jacob
Narrator 1:	Meaning "the heel grabber". [27]The boys grew up. Esau became a man who knew how to hunt, a wanderer in the fields. Jacob was a quiet man, living in tents. [28]Isaac loved Esau because he ate the meat from the hunt. Rebekkah loved Jacob.

ROUND 2: THE BIRTHRIGHT

Narrator 1: [29]Jacob was boiling stew when Esau came from the field. Esau was tired. [30]He said to Jacob:

Esau: Please let me gulp from the red stuff. That red stuff.

Narrator 2: Because of this, they called his name:

They: Edom (meaning the "red one").

Narrator 1: [31]Jacob said:

Jacob: First, sell me your firstborn right.

Esau: [32]I am about to die! What good is the firstborn right to me?

Jacob : [33]Swear it to me.

Narrator 2: He swore and sold his firstborn right to Jacob. [34]Jacob gave Esau bread and boiled beans. Esau ate. He drank. He got up. And he walked away. This is how Esau rejected his firstborn right.

ROUND 3: THE BLESSING

Narrator 1: [27:1]When Isaac was old and his eyes too weak to see, he called for his older son Esau:

Isaac: My son.

Esau: *Hinneini*, I am here.

Isaac: [2]I am old, and I do not know when I will die. [3]Please take your weapons, your arrows and your bow, and go out into the field and hunt me some meat. [4]Make me a tasty treat just the way I love and bring it to me and I will eat. Then I can give you my blessing before I die.

Narrator 2: [5]Rebekkah overheard what Isaac said to Esau his son. Esau went out to the field to hunt game to bring to his father. [6]Rebekkah said to Jacob her son:

I AM A SMOOTH MAN
(GENESIS 27:11)

When Rebekkah tells Jacob to trick his father into giving him the blessing instead of Esau, he says, "I AM A SMOOTH MAN." Then he continues: "MAYBE MY FATHER WILL FEEL ME, AND I WILL BE A TRICKSTER IN HIS EYES AND BRING A CURSE UPON MYSELF, AND NOT A BLESSING.

Everyone reading this assumes that he is talking about not being hairy, but, Rabbi Avreh teaches that he was saying "I am not sharp and cunning, and I will not be able to fulfill this task." Jacob wanted to fail. He did not want to get his father's blessing because of a trick.

Do you agree with this interpretation? Why or why not?

Rebekkah: I heard your father speaking to Esau your brother. He said (her version):

⁷Bring me meat and make me a tasty treat and I will give you Adonai's blessing before I die.

Rebekkah: ⁸Now, my son, listen to my voice and do what I command you. ⁹Go to the herd and take two good kids (young goats). I will make them into a tasty treat for your father, just the way he loves. ¹⁰You will bring it to him. He will eat. And because of this he will bless you before he dies.

Narrator 1: ¹¹Jacob said to Rebekkah his mother:

Jacob: Esau my brother is a hairy man, and **I am a smooth man**. ¹²Maybe my father will feel me, and I will be a trickster in his eyes and bring a curse upon myself, and not a blessing.

Rebekkah: ¹³The curse will be on me, my son. So listen to my voice. Go and get them for me.

Narrator 2: ¹⁴He went, he got them, and he brought them to his mother. His mother made a tasty treat, just the way his father loved. ¹⁵Rebekkah took her older son Esau's clothes, which were with her at home, and dressed Jacob, her younger son. ¹⁶She clothed his hands and the hairless part of his neck with the goats' skins. ¹⁷She put the tasty treat and the bread she made in her son Jacob's hands. ¹⁸He came to his father and said:

JACOB'S BLESSING

Jacob: My father.

Isaac: *Hinneini*, I am here. Which one are you, my son?

Narrator 1: [19]Jacob said to his father,

Jacob: I am Esau your firstborn. I have done what you have told me. Please, sit and eat my game so that you can give me your blessing.

Narrator 2: [20]Isaac said to his son:

Isaac: How is it that you found it so quickly, my son?

Jacob: Adonai your God made it happen for me.

Narrator 1: [21]Isaac said to Jacob:

Isaac: Come close to me and I will feel you, my son, to find out if you are my son Esau or not.

Narrator 2: [22]Jacob came close to Isaac his father. Isaac felt Jacob and said:

Isaac: The voice is the voice of Jacob, but the hands are the hands of Esau.

Narrator 1: [23]Isaac didn't know him, because Jacob's hands were hairy like his brother Esau's hands. Isaac blessed Jacob. [24]He said:

Isaac: You are my son Esau?

Jacob: I am.

Isaac: [25]Come close to me, I will eat from my son's hunted meat, so that I can give your blessing.

Narrator 2: He came close to him. He ate. He brought him wine. He drank. [26]Isaac his father said to him:

Isaac: Please, come close and kiss me, my son.

Narrator 1: [27]Jacob came close and kissed him, and Isaac smelled the smell of his clothes and blessed him.

Isaac: See, the smell of my son is like the smell of a field which Adonai has blessed. [28]May God give you from the dew of the sky and the richness of the earth and much grain and new wine. [29]May nations serve you, and may peoples bow to you. Be master over your brother, and may the sons of your mother bow to you. Let those who curse you be cursed. Let those who bless you be blessed.

ESAU'S BLESSING

Narrator 2: [30]As soon as Isaac finished blessing Jacob, Jacob left Isaac his father. Esau his brother came in with the hunted meat. [31]He had also made tasty food and brought it to his father. He said to his father:

Esau: Get up, my father, and eat from this hunted meat so that you can give me your blessing.

Narrator 1: [32]Isaac his father said to him:

Isaac: Who are you?

Esau: I am your son, your firstborn, Esau.

Narrator 2: [33]Isaac shivered. He said:

Isaac: Who was it who hunted meat, and brought it to me, so that I ate, before you came? I blessed him, and he shall stay blessed.

Narrator 1: [34]When Esau heard his father's words he shouted a great and bitter shout. He said to his father:

Esau: Bless me, too, my father.

Isaac: [35]Your brother came, sneaked in, and took your blessing.

Esau: ³⁶That is why he is named Jacob (meaning "the one who grabs heels"). He has grabbed from me two times. The first time he took my birthright. Here, now, he took my blessing.

Isaac: ³⁷I have made him your master. I gave him your brothers for servants, I gave him corn and new wine. What can I do for you, my son?

Narrator 2: ³⁸Esau said to his father:

Esau: Don't you have one blessing left for me, Father?

Narrator 1: Esau lifted up his voice and cried. Isaac, his father, answered him:

Isaac: ³⁹You will live in the richness of the land. The dew of the sky will be on it. ⁴⁰You will live by the sword and you will serve your brother. But when you fight back, you will break free of him.

Experiences

Do one of these things.

Write Your Own Midrash

Write and perform the scene that takes place the first time that Rebekkah and Esau talk after this story.

Isaac Motivation Debate

One of the big questions about this story is "Does Isaac know that he is really blessing Jacob and not Esau?" Reread the text and stage a debate (or many smaller debates).

Interview God

Why did you set it up as twins? If you want Jacob to be the next patriarch, why not just set him up for the job?

JACOB'S DREAM (GENESIS 28:1–22)

After the encounter with Esau, Jacob leaves home and heads off to "the old country."

Note: Jacob's parents send him to Rebekkah's family to find a wife.

Narrator 1: [28:10]Jacob went out from Be'er Sheva and went towards <u>H</u>aran. [11]He came to a place and camped there when the sun had set. He took one of the stones of the place and put it under his head. He lay down in this place. [12]He dreamed. ***Hinnei* a ladder was set up on earth. Its top reached the sky.** *Hinnei* God's angels were going up and down on it. [13]*Hinnei* God was before him and said:

HINNEI A LADDER WAS SET UP ON EARTH. ITS TOP REACHED THE SKY. (GENESIS 28:12)

A person improves his or her behavior in steps—like on a ladder. Just as a ladder needs steps and a high place to lean against, so does a person need to have steps to achieve and something high to lean against. Righteous people ascend the ladder. (Rabbi Avraham Zalmans) .

What does your ladder look like?

God: I am Adonai, the God of Abraham your father and the God of Isaac. The land on which you are lying, I will give it to you and to your future-family. **Your future-family will be like the dust of the earth.** You will spread out to the sea, and to the east, and to the north, and to the south. All the families of the earth will be blessed through your future-family. *Hinnei* I am with you. I will keep you in all your goings and I will return you to this soil because I will not leave you until I have done all that I promised you.

Narrator 2: Jacob awoke. He said:

Jacob For sure, God is in this place, and I didn't know it.

Narrator 1: He was awestruck. He said:

Jacob: This place is awesome. This is the house of God. This is the gate to heaven.

Narrator 2: Jacob got up early in the morning. He took the stone from under his head. He set it up as a marker and poured oil on it. He called the name of the place

Jacob: Beth-El

Narrator 1: meaning "the house of God", though the original name of that city was Luz. Jacob made a promise:

Jacob: If God will be with me and keep me in this journey on which I am going, and if I am given bread to eat and clothes to wear, and if I return in peace to my father's house, then Adonai will be God to me. This stone which I put as a marker will be the house of God. I will tithe ten percent of everything given to me for You.

Experiences

Do one of these things.

Paper-Tear Midrash

Create your own visual image of this story.

Interview

Imagine that you are a reporter. Rehearse and perform the following interviews.

- Ask Jacob: "What did you think of when you walked from your father's camp to Beth-El?"
- Ask God: "What did the dream of the ladder mean?"
- Ask Jacob: "What did you learn from the dream?"

Write and Perform Your Own Midrash Song

Write the song the angels sang on the ladder between the rungs.

TWO WEDDINGS (GENESIS 29:1–30)

This is the next stop on Jacob's journey.

THE WELL

Narrator 1: [1]Jacob resumed his journey and came to the land of the families of the East. [2]He looked and *hinnei*, a well was in the field, and *hinnei*, there were three flocks of sheep resting by it. From that well the flocks were watered. **A great stone covered the well's mouth**. There all the flocks gathered. The stone was rolled from the well's mouth, and the sheep were watered. Then the stone was put back on the well's mouth in its place. [4]And Jacob said to them:

Jacob: My brothers, where do you come from?

Narrator 1: They said:

Shepherds: We come from <u>H</u>aran.

A GREAT STONE COVERED THE WELL'S MOUTH (GENESIS 29:2)

There was not a lot of water in this location. People were worried that others would get to the water and use it up before they got there. They put a big stone that took all of them to move. That way they felt safe that the water would be shared fairly. (Rabbi Samson Raphael Hirsch)

Why do you think this was a good and fair system?

Narrator 2: He said to them:

Jacob: Do you know Laban, the son of Nahor?

Narrator 1: And they said:

Shepherds: We know him.

Jacob: Is it well with him?

Shepherds: It is well, and *hinnei*, here is Rachel, his daughter, coming with the sheep.

Jacob: There is still a lot of day left. It is not time to gather the cattle together. Water your sheep and go and feed them.

Shepherds: We can't until all the flocks are gathered together. Then all of us roll the stone from the well's mouth. Then we water the sheep.

MEETING DAD

Narrator 1: While he was yet speaking with them, Rachel came with her father's sheep; for she was a shepherdess. It came to pass when Jacob saw Rachel, the daughter of Laban, his mother's brother, and the sheep of Laban...Jacob went and rolled the stone from the well's mouth. He watered the flock of Laban, his mother's brother. Jacob kissed Rachel, lifted up his voice and cried. And Jacob told Rachel that he was her father's relative, that he was Rebekkah's son. She ran and told her father.

Narrator 2: It came to pass, when Laban heard the news about Jacob, his sister's son, he ran to meet him. He hugged him, kissed him, and brought him to his house. He told Laban all the news. Laban said to him:

Laban: You are my bone and my flesh.

Narrator 1: He stayed with them a month. Then Laban said to Jacob:

Laban: Just because you are like a brother to me, why should you serve me for free? Tell me what payment you want.

Narrator 2: Laban had two daughters. The older was named Leah. The younger was named Rachel. Leah had weak eyes. Rachel was nicely shaped and nice to look at. Jacob loved Rachel.

Jacob: I will serve you for seven years for Rachel your younger daughter.

Laban: It is better for me to give her to you than to give her to any other man. Live here with me.

Narrator 1: Jacob served for Rachel for seven years. In his eyes it was just like a few days because he loved her. Jacob said to Laban:

Jacob: Bring me my wife, for my days of labor are completed.

THE FIRST WEDDING

Narrator 1: Laban gathered all the people of the place. He made a party with wine and food. In the evening he took Leah his daughter and brought her to Jacob. (Laban gave his woman-servant, Zilpah, to Leah to be her maid.)

Morning came, and *hinnei*, there was Leah. Jacob said to Laban:

Jacob: What is this you did to me? I served you for Rachel. Why did you trick me?

THE SECOND WEDDING

Laban: **We don't do that in our place. We don't give the younger daughter before the older daughter**. Complete the wedding week and I will give the younger to you, too, as payment for service with me. Serve me another seven years.

Narrator: Jacob did this. After the wedding week Laban gave him Rachel, his daughter, to be his wife. (Laban gave his servant Bilhah to Rachel to be her maid.) Jacob married and loved Rachel more than Leah. He served another seven years.

WE DON'T DO THAT IN OUR PLACE. WE DON'T GIVE THE YOUNGER DAUGHTER BEFORE THE OLDER DAUGHTER (GENESIS 29:29)

When Laban said this he was being sarcastic. He knew that Jacob had taken both the birthright and the blessing from Esau, his older brother. He basically said, "Maybe it is your custom to replace the older with the younger." (Beit ha-Levi)

How do you think Jacob felt when he heard this? Did it bother him or not?

Experiences

Do one of these things.

Dance or Pantomime

Choreograph a dance or a pantomime of the story of how Jacob married two sisters.

Photo Album

Design a photo album for Jacob's family. You may want to dress up and take real pictures. To help you with more details, you will want to add the end of chapter 29 through chapter 30 of Genesis to get the birth of Jacob's children. Decide where you would put people in the family portrait.

Make a Midrash

Zilpah was Leah's handmaiden. Bilhah was Rachel's handmaiden. Write a conversation between the two of them about their mistresses' shared husband.

THE WRESTLING MATCH (GENESIS 32:2–35:17)

After more than twenty years with Laban, Jacob heads for home. Jacob now has two wives, two handmaidens and eleven children.

ANGELS

Narrator 1: ²Jacob went on his way. God's messenger angels met him. When Jacob saw them, he said:

Jacob: This is God's camp.

DIVIDING THE CAMP

Narrator 2: He called the name of the place:

Jacob: *Mahana'im*

Narrator 1: meaning "the camps". **Jacob sent messengers (angels) before him to Esau his brother**. He commanded them, saying:

Jacob: This you shall say to my master, to Esau. "I have lived with Laban, stayed there until now. I have cattle, donkeys, sheep, and servants. I am letting you know this, my master, to find favor in your eyes."

Narrator 2: The messengers returned and said to Jacob:

Messengers: We came to your brother Esau, and he is on his way to meet you. Four hundred men are with him.

Narrator 1: Jacob was very afraid. He split his people and all that he owned into two camps. He said:

Jacob: If Esau comes to one camp and attacks it, perhaps the other camp will escape.

JACOB'S PRAYER

God of my father Abraham and God of my father Isaac, You said to me, "Return to your land, to your birthplace, and I will do good for you." I do not deserve Your mercy. I crossed the Jordan River, and now my camp is split in two. Please save me from the hand of my brother, from the hand of Esau. I am afraid that he will come and kill me, and the mothers with the children.

Narrator 2: He camped that night. He selected gifts from what was at hand for his brother Esau. These he put in the hands of his servants. He said to them:

Jacob: Cross before me...[19]When you see Esau my brother...[20]say, "Your servant Jacob is sending presents to my master. He is behind us."

[21]I will wipe anger from his face by the gift that goes ahead of my face. Later I will see his face, when the gifts have crossed before his face...

THE WRESTLING

Narrator 1: [22]Jacob awoke the same night. He took his two wives and their two servants and his eleven children and crossed them across the Jabbok river. [23]He took them, and crossed them, and had all that was his brought across the river. [24]And Jacob was left alone. And a man wrestled with him until the dawn. [25]When the other saw that he could not win, he touched Jacob's leg and twisted his hip while wrestling with him.

Wrestler: [26]Let me go; the sun is rising.

Jacob: **I won't let you go unless you bless me.**

Wrestler: [27]What is your name?

Jacob: Jacob

Narrator 2: meaning "one who grabs heels".

Wrestler: [28]Jacob is not your name anymore. Israel

Narrator 1: meaning "the one who wrestles with God"

Wrestler: is your name, because you have struggled with God and with people, and you overcame.

I WON'T LET YOU GO UNLESS YOU BLESS ME (GENESIS 32:27)

Jacob was not asking for a new blessing. Instead he was asking the angel to confirm the blessing that his father gave him when he pretended to be Esau. (Rashi)

How do you get blessings?

Jacob: What is your name?

Wrestler: Why do you ask my name?

Narrator 2: He blessed him there. Jacob called the name of the place

Jacob: Peniel

Narrator 1: Meaning "the face of God"

Jacob: Because I have seen God face to face and my life was saved.

Narrator 2: The sun rose over him as he crossed Peniel. He limped on his foot, because of his hip.

THE BROTHERS MEET

Narrator 1: Jacob looked up and saw Esau coming with four hundred men. Jacob spread out his children among Leah, Rachel, and the two maids. He put the maids and their children first. Leah and her children were behind them, and Rachel and Joseph were at the back. He crossed before them and bowed to the ground seven times, until he came close to his brother.

Esau ran to meet him. He hugged him. He kissed him, and they cried. Esau lifted his eyes and saw the women and the children.

Esau: Who are these people with you?

Jacob: The children with whom Adonai has favored your servant.

Narrator 2: Then the maids and their children came close and bowed. Also Leah and her children came close and bowed. Last, Joseph and Rachel came close and bowed. And he said to him:

Esau: Why did I meet your whole camp?

Jacob: To find favor in my master's eyes.

Esau: ¹I have much, my brother. Let what is yours be yours.

Jacob: ¹Please, if I have found favor in your eyes, take this gift from my hand, because when I see your face, it is like seeing the face of God. You have been good to me. ¹Please take this gift of blessing that I brought you, because Adonai has favored me and I have everything.

Narrator 1: He urged him and he took it.

Narrator 2: ¹Esau said:

Esau: Let us travel, and I will go along with you.

Jacob: ¹Know that the children are young, and the sheep and the oxen have newborns. If you drive them hard the flocks will die. ¹My master, please cross ahead of your servant, and I will travel at the speed of the herd and at the speed of the children.

Narrator 1: ¹That day Esau returned to Seir. ¹Jacob traveled to Sukkot. He built himself a house and made sukkot (meaning "booths") for his cattle. That is why the place is called Sukkot.

Experiences

Do one of these things.

Video Your Own Midrash

Have the angel who wrestled Jacob tell the story of his match with Jacob to another angel.

Interviews

Imagine that you are a reporter. Conduct the following interviews.

- Ask Jacob's wrestling partner: "Who are you, and why did you fight Jacob?"
- Ask Jacob: "What did you think when you saw your brother Esau?"
- Ask Esau: "Why were you nice to Jacob after all he did to you?"
- Ask Israel: "What does your new name mean to you?"

Paper-Tear Midrash

Make a paper-tear midrash of one section of this story.

JOSEPH: THE DREAMS COME TRUE (GENESIS 37:2–45:10)

Since the last story Rachel, Joseph's mother, has died giving birth to Benjamin. If most of the stories in the Torah are short stories, then the story of Joseph is a novel.

Narrator 1: ᵗʰⁱˢThis is the family history of Jacob.

PART 1: JOSEPH, THE DREAMER

Narrator 2: Joseph (meaning "the added one") was seventeen years old. He was a shepherd with his brothers… Joseph made bad reports about them to his father. Israel loved Joseph best of all his sons. He made him a robe of many colors.

Narrator 1: When Joseph's brothers saw that his father loved him more than all his brothers, they hated him and could not speak peacefully to him. Joseph dreamed a dream, and he told it to his brothers. This added to their hate. He said to them:

Joseph: Please, hear this dream which I dreamed. We were tying bundles of grain out in the field, when my bundle rose up and your bundles gathered around and bowed to my bundle.

Narrator 1: His brothers said to him:

Brothers: **"Are you going to be a king, being king to us?** Are you going to be a ruler, ruling over us?"

Narrator 2: His dreams and his words added to their hate. He dreamed another dream and told it to his brothers. He said:

Joseph: I dreamed another dream. The sun, the moon, and the stars were bowing down to me.

Narrator 1: When he told it to his father and his brothers, his father scolded him:

Israel: What kind of dream is this you dreamed? Am I, your mother, and your brothers to come and bow down to the ground before you?

"ARE YOU GOING TO BE A KING, BEING KING TO US? ARE YOU GOING TO BE A RULER, RULING OVER US?"

(GENESIS 37.8)

The brothers said, "You want to rule over us, but you will never do so with our free will. That can't happen because we hate you. Do you think you are going to be able to rule over us by force? We will never accept you voluntarily."
(Vilna Gaon)

When you've finished the story, ask yourself, "Did this dream come true? Were the brothers right?"

PART 2: THE BROTHERS PLOT

Narrator 2: ¹¹Israel said to Joseph:

Israel: Your brothers are tending the sheep in Shechem. Come, I will send you to them.

Joseph: *Hinneini*, I am here.

Israel: ¹⁴Please go and check on your brothers and check on the sheep. Then return and tell me.

Narrator 1: Joseph went after his brothers and found them in Dothan. ¹⁸They saw him coming. Before he could get close, they plotted against him to kill him. ¹⁹The brothers said to each other:

Brothers: Here, the master of dreams is coming. ²⁰Let us kill him and throw him in a pit and say a wild animal ate him. Then we'll see if his dreams come true.

Narrator 2: ²¹Reuben heard this and tried to save him. He said:

Reuben: Let us not take his life. ²²Spill no blood. Throw him in this pit in the wilderness, but don't lay a hand on him.

Narrator 1: This was so that he could save him from their hands and return him to his father.

²³When Joseph came to his brothers they stripped off his robe of many colors, grabbed him, ²⁴and threw him in the pit. ²⁵Then they sat down to eat bread.

Narrator 2: They looked up and saw a caravan of Ishmaelites coming from Gilead. Their camels were carrying gum, balm, and perfume, and they were going down to Egypt. ²⁶Judah said to his brothers:

Judah: **What do we get out of killing our brother and hiding his blood?** Let's sell him to the Ishmaelites, and our hands will not murder. He is our brother and of our flesh.

Narrator 1: They grabbed Joseph, pulled him up from the pit, and sold him to the Ishmaelites for twenty shekels of silver. They brought Joseph to Egypt.

Reuben came back to the pit. Joseph was not in the pit. Reuben tore his robe. He returned to his brothers and said:

Reuben: The boy is gone. What is going to happen to me?

Narrator 2: They butchered a goat and dipped Joseph's robe in the blood. They brought the robe of many colors to their father and said:

Brothers: We found this. Do you recognize it? Is this your son's robe?

Narrator 1: He recognized it and said:

Israel: My son's robe! A wild beast has torn Joseph to pieces and eaten him.

Narrator 2: Jacob tore his robe and mourned his son.

PART 3: JOSEPH IN POTIPHAR'S HOUSE

Narrator 1: ³⁹¹Joseph was taken down to Egypt. Potiphar, Pharaoh's chief overseer, bought him from the hands of the Ishmaelites. ²**Adonai was with Joseph. He was a man who succeeded.** He lived in the house of his Egyptian master.

Narrator 2: ³His master discovered that Adonai was with Joseph when everything placed in Joseph's hands succeeded. ⁴Joseph found favor in his eyes. Joseph personally served him. Everything that was his, he put in Joseph's hands. ⁵Adonai blessed this Egyptian's house because of Joseph.

Narrator 1: ⁶Joseph was nicely shaped and nice to look at. ⁷His master's wife set her eyes on Joseph and said:

Potiphar's Wife: Love me.

Narrator 2: ⁸He refused. He said to his master's wife:

Joseph: My master has put everything in my hands, and he doesn't know what is happening in the house. You are his wife. How could I do such a great evil as this and sin against God?

Narrator 1: ¹⁰She would ask Joseph every day, and he paid no attention to her. ¹¹One such day he came into the house to do his work. No one else was at home. ¹²She grabbed his robe, saying:

Potiphar's Wife: Love me.

ADONAI WAS WITH JOSEPH. HE WAS A MAN WHO SUCCEEDED (GENESIS 39.2)

Usually when a person succeeds he or she takes credit for the success. But Joseph knew that his success came from God. There, even when he succeeded, God was with him. (*Sha'ari Simhah*)

How does God help with success?

Narrator 2: ⁽¹²⁾He left his robe in her hand and ran away. ⁽¹³⁾She called for the household slaves.

Potiphar's Wife: The Hebrew slave came to touch me. ⁽¹⁵⁾When I raised my voice and screamed, he left his robe and ran away…

PART 4: JOSEPH IN JAIL

Narrator 1: ⁽¹⁹⁾When his master heard his wife's story, he burned with anger. ⁽²⁰⁾He threw Joseph in the king's dungeon. ⁽²¹⁾Even in the dungeon, Adonai was with Joseph. Joseph found favor in the eyes of the dungeon-master.

Narrator 2: ⁽²²⁾The dungeon-master put in Joseph's hands all the prisoners and all that was done there. ⁽²³⁾The dungeon-master didn't need to check on anything Joseph did, because Adonai was with him. Everything he did, Adonai made succeed.

Narrator 1: ⁽⁴⁰:¹⁾**It happened after these things that the butler of the king of Egypt and his baker angered their master, Pharaoh, the king of Egypt**. ⁽²⁾Pharaoh was angry with his two officers, with the chief butler and with the chief baker. ⁽³⁾He put them under guard, under the dungeon-master, in the prison, the place where Joseph was imprisoned.

Narrator 2: ⁽⁴⁾And the dungeon-master ordered Joseph to be with them. He served them, and they continued a long

DELVING DEEPER

IT HAPPENED AFTER THESE THINGS THAT THE BUTLER OF THE KING OF EGYPT AND HIS BAKER ANGERED THEIR MASTER, PHARAOH, THE KING OF EGYPT (GENESIS 40:1)

A fly was found in the butler's wine (Rashi). Sometimes the smallest things can bring about great events. It was because of that fly that Joseph came to Pharaoh's attention and began his rise to governor. Jewish history depends on that fly.

(Hillel Zeitlin)

When a butterfly flaps its wings in China it can cause a hurricane to hit South Florida.

(Edward Lorenz)

What is a small thing that became big in your life?

time under guard. And they both dreamed a dream, each his own dream, that same night. The next morning they were sad. Joseph asked them what was wrong. They told him:

Butler & Baker: We dreamed dreams, and there is no one to tell us what they mean.

Narrator 1: Joseph said to them:

Joseph: Don't meanings come from God? Tell me the dreams.

Butler: I saw a grapevine with three branches. Before my eyes the buds turned into flowers, and the grapes became ripe. I took the grapes and made wine for Pharaoh's cup. Then I gave the cup to Pharaoh.

Joseph: In three days, Pharaoh will bring you back to be his butler again.

Narrator 2: Joseph said to him:

Joseph: At the right time, remember me. Please do what is right by me. Remind Pharaoh about me, and take me out of this dungeon. I was stolen from the land of the Hebrews, and here I am innocent, yet they put me in this pit.

Narrator 1: Next the baker told his dream:

Baker: I had three baskets of bread on my head. In the top basket were baked goods for Pharaoh. Birds came and ate from the basket.

Joseph: In three days, Pharaoh will have you killed.

Narrator 2: Three days later was Pharaoh's birthday. He had the butler return to his job, and the baker he had killed. The dreams came true, just as Joseph explained. But the butler forgot about Joseph.

NEXT SEVEN SKINNY COWS CAME OUT, STOOD BY THE OTHER CATTLE, AND ATE THE FAT COWS (GENESIS 41:3—4)

The skinny cows stand for the *yetzer ha-ra* (evil urge) that is hungry. They did three things: (a) came out, (b) stood by, and (c) ate. These are the three stages of the evil urge. It comes out and sees what a person is doing, stands by and becomes his or her friend, and then swallows the victim completely. We are told (Sukkah 52) that the evil urge comes in as a guest and winds up owning the house. (Sefat Emet)

How does your evil urge work?

PART 5: PHARAOH'S DREAMS

Narrator 1: ⁴¹Two years later, Pharaoh had a dream. He dreamed about standing by the Nile ²and seeing seven fat cows come out to graze. **Next, seven skinny cows came out, stood by the other cattle, and ⁴ate the fat cows.** Pharaoh woke up.

⁵When he fell back to sleep, he had a second dream. Seven good ears of grain were growing on one stalk. ⁶Behind them were seven thin and dry ears of grain. ⁷The seven thin ears ate the good ears.

⁸No one could explain Pharaoh's dreams. Not even his magicians, not even his wise men knew what they meant. ⁹Then the chief butler spoke to Pharaoh, saying:

Butler: Today I must mention my faults. ¹⁰Pharaoh was angry with his servants and put me under guard in the house of the dungeon-master, me and the chief baker. ¹¹And we dreamed dreams one night, I and he, each one dreaming his own dream. ¹²And there was with us a young man, a Hebrew, servant to the dungeon-master, and we told him, and he interpreted our dreams to us. To each one according to his dream did he interpret. ¹³And it happened just as he interpreted. I was restored to my office, and he (the baker) was hanged.

Narrator 2: Pharaoh sent for Joseph. They hurried him from the pit. His hair was cut. His clothing was changed. He was brought to Pharaoh. Pharaoh said to Joseph:

Pharaoh: I have dreamed a dream, and there is no one to tell me what it means. I have heard about you. It is said that you know the meaning of dreams.

Narrator 1: Joseph answered Pharaoh:

Joseph: Not I. God will answer for Pharaoh's peace.

Narrator 2: Joseph said to Pharaoh:

Joseph: Pharaoh's dreams, they are one. God has told Pharaoh what will happen. The seven good cows are seven years. The seven good ears of grain are seven years. They are one dream. The seven skinny cows that followed are seven years. The seven thin ears of grain are seven years of famine. What I have told Pharaoh is what God has shown you will happen. Seven years of plenty are coming to the land of Egypt. And they will be followed by seven years of famine. Pharaoh had two dreams because this thing is true. It came from God, and God will quickly do it. Now, let Pharaoh pick a true and wise person and put him in charge of the land of Egypt. Let Pharaoh appoint managers over the land during the seven years of plenty. Collect all kinds of food from the good years to come and store it and keep it. This food will be for the seven bad years which will come. No one in the land of Egypt will die from the famine.

Narrator 1: The plan was good in Pharaoh's eyes. Pharaoh said:

Pharaoh: How can we find another person like this who has the spirit of God in him?

Narrator 2: Pharaoh said to Joseph:

Pharaoh: Since God made all this known to you, no one could be as true and wise as you. You will be over my house. You will command my people. Only because of my throne will I be greater than you. See, I give you all of the land of Egypt.

Narrator 1: Pharaoh took the signet ring off his hand and put it on Joseph's. He dressed him in robes of fine linen and placed a gold chain around his neck.

Narrator 2: The people of Egypt followed Joseph's plan. They stored food during the seven good years… Then the bad years came.

Meanwhile, Joseph married and had two sons named Manasseh and Ephraim. The years of hunger came.

The famine was everywhere. Joseph opened all the storehouses and gave shares of grain to the Egyptians. There was great hunger in Egypt. From all the earth people came to Egypt to get food from Joseph. There was great hunger everywhere.

PART 6: THE FAMILY COMES TO EGYPT

Narrator 1: Ten of Joseph's brothers went down to Egypt to get food. But Jacob didn't send Benjamin, saying,

Jacob: Something might happen to harm him.

Narrator 2: The children of Israel were among those who came to Egypt because of the famine in the land of Canaan. Joseph's brothers came and bowed to the ground before him. When Joseph saw his brothers, he recognized them but treated them as strangers. He spoke to them harshly:

Joseph: Where did you come from?

Brothers: From the land of Canaan, to get food.

Narrator 1: Joseph remembered the dream which he dreamed. Joseph said to his brothers:

Joseph: You are spies.

Narrator 2: They denied it. To prove that they were not spies, they told him the story of the whole family.

Brothers: We are twelve sons of one man, but the youngest son is still with his father, and the other one is no more.

Narrator 1: Joseph wanted to test them. He asked them to bring the youngest son down to Egypt. He had them locked up for three days. There the brothers talked.

Brother: This is happening as punishment for what we did to Joseph.

Reuben: I told you not to harm the boy.

Narrator 2: Joseph heard this and could understand them, even though they thought he couldn't speak their language.

Narrator 1: Joseph went and cried. At the end of the three days Joseph gave them bags of grain but hid their money in the bags. He sent nine of them back to his father and kept Simeon in Egypt, to make sure that they would return.

JOSEPH COULDN'T CONTROL HIMSELF. HE ORDERED: "EVERYONE LEAVE ME" (GENESIS 45:1)

Some people thought that Joseph didn't want to cry in public, but that was not the case. Joseph had pushed his brothers hard so that they would have the chance to understand their sins and repent. He sent everyone else away so that they would not know of his brothers' embarrassment. (Z. Ron)

How did Joseph give his brothers the chance to know their sins against him)?

Narrator 2: The famine was still bad. Even though they didn't want to go back to Egypt, the brothers had no choice. Judah talked Jacob into letting them take Benjamin back with them. When Joseph saw Benjamin, he invited the brothers to eat dinner with him. They were afraid because of the money that was returned, but Joseph's servant explained:

Servant: ⁴⁵²³Be at peace. Don't be afraid. Your God and the God of your fathers gave you a treasure in your sacks.

Narrator 1: First Simeon came in and then Joseph. The brothers bowed to the ground before him a second time. When Joseph met Benjamin he cried, but he hid his tears from his brothers. He washed his face, and the food was served.

Narrator 2: Once again he sent the brothers back to Canaan with bags of grain. This time he hid a silver cup in Benjamin's bag. At the border the brothers were stopped, the silver cup discovered, and they were brought back before Joseph.

Judah came close to him:

Judah: My master, please let your servant speak to you. Don't get angry at your servant, because you are like Pharaoh to him. Now if I come to my father, your servant, and the boy is not with us, he will die. Your servant pledged to my father about the boy. If I do not bring him back, I will have sinned before my father."

Now please let me, your servant, be a slave to you instead of the boy. Let the boy go up with his brothers.

Narrator 1: **Joseph couldn't control himself. He ordered:**

Joseph: Everyone leave me.

Narrator 2: When no one else was there, Joseph made himself known to his brothers. He lifted his voice and cried. Egypt heard him. Pharaoh's house heard him. Joseph said to his brothers:

Joseph: I am Joseph. Is my father still alive?

Narrator 1: His brothers were too surprised to answer. Joseph said:

Joseph: Please come close to me.

Narrator 2: They came close, and he said:

Joseph: I am Joseph your brother, the one you sold into Egypt. Now do not be pained. Do not feel guilty that you sold me. God sent me before you to save life. Hurry, go up to my father and say to him: "God put Joseph your son as master over all Egypt. Come down to me. Settle in the land of Goshen and be near me."

Experiences

Do one of these things.

Make a Storyboard

A storyboard is like a cartoon that is made to show what will happen before a movie is

shot. Break your class into six groups. Have each group draw three to five panels to show what happens in their part of the story. Present the storyboards to the class in order and then hang them around the room.

Coat of Many Colors

Design a coat of many colors. Stripes would be cheating.

Make a *P'Shat* Video

P'shat means "plain Torah" without anything extra. Break into six groups and have groups perform each of the six sections. Collect props and costumes and maybe make backgrounds to make this more fun.

Interview

Imagine that you are a reporter. Conduct the following interviews.

- Ask Joseph's brothers: "When Joseph was a boy, what did you think of him?"
- Ask Joseph's brothers: "Now that the story is over, what do you think of Joseph?"
- Ask Jacob: "Tell me about Joseph."
- Ask Potiphar: "Tell me about Joseph."
- Ask the dungeon-master: "Tell me about Joseph."
- Ask Pharaoh: "Tell me about Joseph."

THE NEW KING (EXODUS 1:1–22)

We have moved from the book of Genesis into the book of Exodus. The previous generation is dead. Israel's family has now grown into a people.

PROLOGUE

Narrator 1: [1]**These are the names of the Families-of-Israel who came to Egypt with Jacob.** Each man came with a household:

Narrator 2: Reuben, Simeon, Levi, and Judah. Issachar, Zebulun, and Benjamin. Dan and Naphtali, Gad and Asher.

THESE ARE THE NAMES OF THE FAMILIES-OF-ISRAEL WHO CAME TO EGYPT WITH JACOB (EXODUS 1:1)

The actual Hebrew says הַבָּאִים ha-ba'im, "who come" to Egypt, not "who came" to Egypt. When people move to a new country they keep their old identity for a while. Eventually they become assimilated and moves into the new culture. Here the Torah uses the present tense to tell us that the Jews were always newcomers in Egypt. They never gave up their own identity. (Rabbi Y.Y. Tronk of Kutno)

What are some active parts of your Jewish identity?

85

Narrator 1: Jacob's family grew to seventy people. Joseph was already in Egypt. Joseph died along with his brothers and all the people of that generation. The children of Israel were fruitful. They increased. They became many. They became very strong. They filled the land.

NEW KING

Narrator 1: There rose a new king over Egypt. He said to his people:

Pharaoh: "Here the nation of the Children of Israel are many and stronger than we. Let's outsmart them, because if there is a war, they might join our enemies and fight against us and leave this land."

THE OPPRESSION

Narrator 2: The Egyptians put taskmasters over them to make them suffer while they worked. The Children of Israel built the cities of Pithom and Raamses. The more the Egyptians made them suffer, the more they multiplied and the more they spread out.

Narrator 1: The Egyptians were afraid of the Children of Israel. The Egyptians made slaves of the Children of Israel. They made their life bitter with hard slavery, slaving with cement and bricks and in the fields.

THE MIDWIVES

Narrator 2: The king of Egypt spoke to the Hebrews' midwives. They were named Shiphrah and Puah. He said:

Pharaoh: "When you help the Hebrew women deliver a baby and you see that it is a boy, kill it. If it is a girl, she may live."

Narrator 1: [17]The midwives were in awe of God and did not do what the king of Egypt told them to do.

Narrator 2: [18]The king of Egypt called for the midwives. He said to them:

Pharaoh: "Why did you let the children live?"

Narrator 2: [19]The midwives said to Pharaoh:

Shifrah and Puah: "Hebrew women aren't like Egyptian women. They have easy deliveries, and sometimes their children are born before the midwife arrives."

Narrator 1: [20]God made it good for the midwives. [21]**Because the midwives were in awe of God, God made them mothers of great families**.

GENOCIDE

Narrator 2: [22]Pharaoh commanded his whole people:

Egyptians: "Every Hebrew son that is born you will throw into the river. The daughters can live."

BECAUSE THE MIDWIVES WERE IN AWE OF GOD, GOD MADE THEM MOTHERS OF GREAT FAMILIES (EXODUS 1:21)

When a person fears another person she cannot remain calm. When a person is in awe/fear of God, it brings calm to the soul. Because the midwives were in awe of God, God made them fearless and calm. They were not afraid of Pharaoh's decrees. God's made them great, calm mothers as a reward. (Mei ha-Shilo'a<u>h</u>)

What's your relationship with God like?

Experiences

Do one of these things.

Act It Out

Either write or improvise a grandparent telling his or her grandchildren about what life was like under the old Pharaoh who knew Joseph, and how it changed under the new Pharaoh who didn't know Joseph.

Biography

There is an argument in the midrash about who the midwives were. Some say they were Jews. Some say they were non–Jews. Solve the problem by writing a biography of the two midwives who were named Shifrah and Pu'ah.

Genealogy

Form groups. Imagine you are a member of a Jewish family that is enslaved in Egypt. Trace your genealogy back to Abraham and Sarah.

MEET MOSES (EXODUS 2:1–22)

The story continues directly on.

PART 1: MOSES IS BORN

Narrator 1: **A man from the tribe of Levi married a daughter of the tribe of Levi.** The woman became pregnant and gave birth to a son. She saw that he was good. She hid him for three months. When she was no longer able to hide him she took an ark of bulrushes, covered it with slime and tar, put him in it, and put it in the reeds on the bank of the Nile.

Narrator 2: His sister watched from a distance to know what would happen to him. Pharaoh's daughter came down to the Nile to bathe. She saw the ark in the reeds and sent her servant to get it. She opened it and saw a child, a boy, crying. She felt pity for him. She said:

A MAN FROM THE TRIBE OF LEVI MARRIED A DAUGHTER OF THE TRIBE OF LEVI (EXODUS 2:1)

Why doesn't the Torah mention the husband's (Amram) or the wife's (Yoheved) name? This is because the Torah wanted to show that the redeemer could come out of any home or any family. (Sefer Yuhasen)

How is your family a source of redemption? What are you bringing to the fixing of the world?

Pharaoh's Daughter: This is a Hebrew child.

Narrator 1: Then his sister said to Pharaoh's daughter:

Miriam: Shall I go and call a Hebrew woman to nurse the child for you?

Narrator 2: Pharaoh's daughter said to her:

Pharaoh's Daughter: Go.

Narrator 2: She went and called the child's mother. Pharaoh's daughter said to the mother:

Pharaoh's Daughter: Go and take this child. Nurse him, and I will pay you.

Narrator 1: The woman took the child and nursed him. The child grew up. The mother took him to Pharaoh's daughter. He became her son. She named him Moses, saying:

Pharaoh's Daughter: Moses means I drew him from the water.

PART 2: MOSES SEES

Narrator 1: When Moses grew up he went out to his brothers. He saw their suffering. He saw an Egyptian man beating a Hebrew man—one of his brothers. **He looked this way and that way.** No one was around. He killed the Egyptian and hid him in the sand.

HE LOOKED THIS WAY AND THAT WAY. NO ONE WAS AROUND (EXODUS 2.12)

Moses looked around Egypt and saw that Jews were considered to be "no one." They weren't thought of as human. Everything he had tried to accomplish within the Pharaoh's house did nothing. He was left taking action on his own. (Rabbi Meir Shapira of Lublin)

What do you do when you see people being treated as "no one"?

Narrator 2: ¹¹He went out the next day. Two Hebrew men were fighting. He said to the guilty one:

Moses: Why are you beating your neighbor?

Narrator 2: ¹⁴He said:

Hebrew: Who made you our boss and our judge? Do you want to kill me, too, just as you killed the Egyptian?

Narrator 1: Moses was afraid. He said:

Moses: The thing is known.

Narrator 1: ¹⁵When Pharaoh learned of this, he wanted to kill Moses.

PART 3: MOSES FLEES TO MIDIAN

Narrator 2: Moses escaped. He came to settle in the land of Midian. He sat by a well. ¹⁶The priest of Midian had seven daughters. They came and drew water for their father's sheep. ¹⁷Some shepherds came and drove them away. Moses stood up and saved them. He gave water to their sheep.

Narrator 1: ¹⁸When they came to their father, he said:

Jethro: How did you manage to come home so quickly today?

Narrator 1: They said to him:

Daughters: ¹⁹An Egyptian man saved us from the hand of the shepherds. He also drew water many times for us and gave water to the sheep."

Narrator 1: ²⁰He said to his daughters:

Jethro: Where is this man? How could you leave him? Call him, and he will eat with us.

Narrator 2: ²¹Moses was happy to stay with the man. One daughter, Zipporah, became Moses' wife. ²²She gave birth to a son. He named his son

Moses: Gershom (meaning "the stranger").

Narrator 2: He said:

Moses: I have been a stranger in a strange land.

Experiences

Do one of these things.

Stranger in a Strange Land

Write a song or rap about Moses. Use "Stranger in a strange land" as the chorus.

Video the Wedding of Moses and Zipporah

Zipporah's father Yitro was the High Priest of Midian. He would have been the one to perform the marriage. Make a wedding video for the two.

Try Moses for Killing the Egyptian

Is Moses a murderer or a hero? Stage the trial with witnesses, opening and closing statements, etc.

THE BURNING BUSH (EXODUS 2:23–3:12)

This is the next piece of Torah. Here is the text of this story.

²³The king of Egypt died. The Children of Israel were groaning from slaving. They cried out, and their cry came up to God. ²⁴God heard them. God remembered the covenant with Abraham, with Isaac, and with Jacob. ²⁵God saw the Children of Israel. God knew.

^{3:1}Moses was tending his father-in-law Jethro's sheep. He led the sheep into the wilderness and came to Horeb, the Mountain of God. ²An angel of God appeared to him in the flame of a burning bush. He saw the bush was burning but not burnt by the flames. ³Moses said: "I must turn aside to see this wonderful sight. Why isn't the bush burnt?"

⁴Adonai saw that he turned aside. **God called to him from the bush: "Moses, Moses."**

He said: "*Hinneini*/I am here."

GOD CALLED TO HIM FROM THE BUSH: "MOSES, MOSES" (EXODUS 3:4)

The Jewish people never completely believed in Moses. They were never totally sure that the signs and wonders that he did were not really magic. Anyone who sees things that do not happen normally is somewhat doubtful about witnessing God's work rather than an illusion. In the wilderness Moses only did miracles when the Families-of-Israel had needs. He brought water when they needed water, brought food when they needed food. At Mount Sinai the Torah tells us that God says, "Hinneini/Here I am, coming to you in a thick cloud so that everyone can hear when I speak to you, and so that they may believe you forever..." It shows that even there the people needed convincing that Moses worked for God. (Maimonides, *Yesodei ha-Torah* 8:1)

Do you believe that Moses and God really did miracles in Egypt?

93

I HAVE SEEN AND SEEN AGAIN THE SUFFERING OF MY PEOPLE IN EGYPT (EXODUS 3:7)

Every other time that the Jewish people went into exile they were spread out all over the world. Only in Egypt were they in exile together, in Goshen. Egypt was the only exile before the giving of the Torah. Without the Torah the Jewish people would never hold together. But now that we have the Torah we can be spread all over the world and still be one people. (Rabbi Avraham of Sohahew)

What do you believe holds the Jewish people together?

God said: "Don't come close. First take off your sandals. This place where you are standing is holy ground.

I am the God of your fathers, the God of Abraham, the God of Isaac, and the God of Jacob."

Moses hid his face because he was afraid to look at God. Adonai said: **"I have seen and seen again the suffering of My people in Egypt.** I have heard their cry; I know their pain. I have come down to save them from the hands of the Egyptians and to bring them up to land both good and wide, to a land of milk and honey, to Canaan…Now I am sending you to Pharaoh, and you will bring My people, the Children-of-Israel, out from Egypt."

Moses said: "Who am I, that I should go to Pharaoh? Who am I, that I should bring out the Families-of-Israel?"

God said: "I will be with you. Let this be a sign for you, for I have sent you. When you bring the people out of Egypt, all of you will serve Adonai at this very mountain."

Create your own script for this story. Feel free to play with the translation.

Narrator: 2:23 _____

_____

24 _____

_____

25 _____

_____

_____

3:1 _____

_____

2 _____

_____

_____

Moses: 3 _____?

Narrator: 4 _____

God: _____

Narrator: _____

_____

Moses: _____

Narrator: [5]_____

God: _____

_____

_____

Narrator: _____

[7]_____

_____

God: _____

_____

_____

_____

_____

_____

Narrator: [11]_____

Moses: _____

_____

_____

Narrator: [12] _____

God: _____

_____

Experiences

Do one of these things.

Paper-Tear Midrash

Create your interpretation of the burning bush moment.

Interviews

Imagine you are a reporter.

- Interview God: "How could you go so many years without acknowledging the suffering of the Families-of-Israel?"

- Interview Moses: "What was it like at the burning bush? Can you tell us more about it?"

- Also ask God: "Why did you pick Moses?"

Moses' Diary

Write a diary entry for Moses talking about how he feels about being sent back to Egypt.

CROSSING THE REED SEA (EXODUS 14:1–31, 15:1, 15:11, 15:20)

We have skipped the plagues, the seder in Egypt, the baking of matzah and all of the events that began with Moses' return and led to the actual Exodus. We are now on the banks of the Reed Sea.

PRELUDE

Narrator 1: ¹Then Adonai said to Moses:

God: ²"Tell the people of Israel to turn back and camp in front of Pi ha-Ḥirot, between Migdol and the sea, in front of Baal Zephon; you should camp next to the sea. ³For Pharaoh will say of the Families-of-Israel:

Pharaoh: They are caught in the land; the wilderness has shut them in.

God: ·And I will harden Pharaoh's heart, and he will pursue them, and I will get glory over Pharaoh and all his army; and the Egyptians shall know that I am Adonai.

Narrator 2: And they did so. ·When the king of Egypt was told that the people had fled, the heart of Pharaoh and his servants was changed toward the people, and they said, "What is this we have done, that we have let Israel go from serving us?" ·So he made ready his chariot and took his army with him ·and all the chariots of Egypt.... ·And Adonai hardened the heart of Pharaoh, king of Egypt, and he chased the Families-of-Israel as they proudly left. ·The Egyptians chased them, all Pharaoh's horses and chariots and his horsemen and his army, and overtook them camped at the sea... ·When Pharaoh drew near, the people of Israel lifted up their eyes, and *hinnei*, the Egyptians were marching after them. They were very afraid. And the Families-of-Israel cried out to Adonai.

CONFRONTATION

Narrator 1: ·And they said to Moses,

Israel: Is it because there are no graves in Egypt that you have taken us away to die in the wilderness? What have you done to us, bringing us out of Egypt? · Is not this what we said to you in Egypt, "Let us alone and let us serve the Egyptians"? For it would have been better for us to serve the Egyptians than to die in the wilderness.

Narrator 2: ¹³Moses said to the people,

Moses: Don't be afraid. Stand firm. See the salvation of Adonai that God will do for you today. The Egyptians whom you see today, you will never see again…

Narrator 1: ¹⁵Adonai said to Moses:

GET GOING

God **Why waste time crying to me? Tell the people of Israel to get going.** ¹⁶Lift up your rod and stretch out your hand over the sea and divide it, that the Families-of-Israel may go on dry ground through the sea. ¹⁷I will harden the hearts of the Egyptians so that they shall go in after them, and I will get glory over Pharaoh and all his army, his chariots, and his horsemen. ¹⁸And the Egyptians shall know that I am Adonai when I have gotten glory over Pharaoh, his chariots, and his horsemen…

Narrator 2: ²¹Then Moses stretched out his hand over the sea; and Adonai drove the sea back by a strong east wind all night, and made the sea dry land, and the waters were divided. ²²And the Families-of-Israel walked into the middle of the sea on dry ground, the waters being a wall to them on their right hand and on their left. ²³The Egyptians chased and went in after them into the middle of the sea, all Pharaoh's horses, his chariots, and his horsemen…

WHY WASTE TIME CRYING TO ME? TELL THE PEOPLE OF ISRAEL TO GET GOING (EXODUS 14:15)

Why was Moses crying out to God? Didn't he know that God would keep God's promise to take the Jews out of Egypt? Rather, Moses' love of his fellow Jews was so great that when he saw how much they were suffering, he lost his patience and couldn't keep himself from expressing what he felt.

What do you do when you see people suffering?

Narrator 1: Then Adonai said to Moses:

God: Stretch out your hand over the sea that the water may come back upon the Egyptians, upon their chariots, and upon their horsemen.

Narrator 2: So Moses stretched forth his hand over the sea, and the sea returned to its usual flow… The waters returned and covered the chariots and the horsemen and all the army of Pharaoh that had followed them into the sea; not so much as one of them remained. But the Families-of-Israel walked on dry ground through the sea, the waters being a wall to them on their right hand and on their left. Thus Adonai saved Israel that day from the hand of the Egyptians; and Israel saw the Egyptians dead upon the seashore. Israel saw the great work that Adonai did against the Egyptians, and the people feared Adonai; and they believed in Adonai and in God's servant Moses.

MOSES LEADS SINGING

Narrator 1: Then Moses and the Families-of-Israel sang this song to Adonai, saying,

Israel: I will sing to Adonai, for God has triumphed gloriously; the horse and rider God has thrown into the sea… Who is like You, Adonai among the gods? Who is like You, majestic in holiness, awesome in glorious deeds, doing wonders?

MIRIAM LEADS SINGING

Narrator 2: "Then Miriam, the prophetess, the sister of Aaron, took a timbrel in her hand, and all the women went out after her with timbrels and dancing.

Experiences

Do one of these things.

Claymation

Use Plasticine clay and create a series of images of the crossing of the Reed Sea. Take photographs of your model in action. Use your pictures to create a storyboard with captions.

Song Session

Split your class into two groups, boys in one and girls in the other. Have each group write a song that they believe Israel sang at the Reed Sea. Have them perform their songs to each other.

Debate

Divide the class into two groups. Have one group be the people who want to go back to Egypt. Have the other group be the people who want to go with Moses. Have the groups argue one on one with each other.

THE TEN COMMANDMENTS (EXODUS 19:1–10, 19:17, 20:1–14)

We have skipped Moses hitting a rock and getting water and a battle with Amalek. Three months have gone by, and we have now come to Mount Sinai.

GETTING READY

Narrator 1: [19]Three months after the Families-of-Israel exited Egypt they came to the wilderness of Sinai. [2]Israel camped before that mountain. [3]Moses climbed up to God and Adonai called to him from the mountain:

God: Say this to the house of Jacob and tell this to the Families-of-Israel. **You have seen what I did to the Egyptians, and how I carried you on eagles' wings and brought you to Me.** Now, if you will listen to my voice and keep my covenant and be my treasure from among all peoples, then you shall be to Me a kingdom of priests and a holy nation…

Narrator 2: Moses came and called for the elders of the people. He set before them all the words that Adonai had commanded him. The whole people answered together:

Families-of-Israel: All that Adonai said, we will do.

Narrator 1: Moses reported all the people's words to Adonai. Adonai said to Moses:

God: *Hinnei*/Here I am, coming to you in a thick cloud so that everyone can hear when I speak to you, and so that they may believe you forever…

Narrator 2: Moses brought the people from the camp to meet God. They stood at the bottom of the mountain. Mount Sinai was all smoke because Adonai came down in fire. The smoke rose like the smoke of a furnace. The whole mountain shook. Adonai said all these things:

THE TEN COMMANDMENTS

God: 1. ¹I am Adonai your God, who brought you out of the land of Egypt, out of slavery.

2. ²You will not have any other gods before Me. ³You will not make any idols. ⁴Do not bow down to idols or serve them.

3. ⁷Do not use the name of Adonai, your God, when making a false promise.

4. ⁸Remember the Shabbat. Make it holy. ⁹You may labor for six days and do all your work. ¹⁰But the seventh day is Shabbat.

5. ¹²Honor your father and your mother.

6. ¹³Do not murder.

7. ¹⁴Do not commit adultery.

8. ¹⁵**Do not steal.**

9. ¹⁶Do not lie about your neighbor in an oath.

10. ¹⁷Do not wish to take over your neighbor's house or anything that belongs to your neighbor.

DO NOT STEAL (EXODUS 20:15)

The Torah doesn't make a list of things not to steal. It means to teach us not to steal anything: money, opinions, or even time. Lying is a kind of stealing. (Shakh)

List some other kinds of theft.

Experiences

Do one of these things.

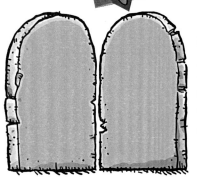

Cut Your Own Tablets

Make your own Ten Commandments paperweight out of clay. Your teacher will help you find the first Hebrew word of each commandment. Write down one or two words to stand for each of the commandments.

Find Out the Connection

Look at the difference between the Jewish Ten Commandments and the Christian Ten Commandments. You may need to use the Internet to help you find the difference. Then look at the connection between the first five commandments and the second five. According to the Jewish tradition, the first five are between people and God; the second five are between people and people. Also, commandment one is supposed to connect with commandment six, two with seven, etc.

Make It One Commandment

Various teachers have tried to reduce the Ten Commandments to one commandment. Break into groups and see if you can figure out one catch-all commandment.

THE HOLINESS CODE (LEVITICUS 19:1–4, 9–18)

We have jumped into the middle of Leviticus. We have skipped lots of rules, the building of the Tabernacle and a lot of complaining by Israel.

Narrator 1: ¹ᵇ¹And Adonai said to Moses, saying:

God: ²Say to all of the community of the Families-of-Israel, **You shall be holy; for I, Adonai, your God, am holy**.

³Every one of you shall be in awe of his mother and her father, and you shall keep my shabbatot: I am Adonai, your God.

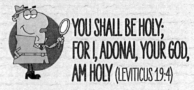

YOU SHALL BE HOLY; FOR I, ADONAI, YOUR GOD, AM HOLY (LEVITICUS 19:4)

This command is written in the future tense. God doesn't expect us to start out holy. Rather, God expects us to get holier and holier as we grow and learn, as we make mistakes and fix them. (Maimonides, *Laws of Repentence* 7:5)

What are some ways you have gotten holier?

109

Do not turn to idols or make for yourselves molten gods: I am Adonai, your God.

When you cut down the harvest of your land, you shall not cut down your field to its very borders; neither shall you gather the fallen after your harvest.

And you shall not strip your vineyard bare, nor gather the fallen grapes of your vineyard; you shall leave them for the poor and for the stranger: I am Adonai, your God.

You shall not steal, nor deal falsely, nor lie to one another.

And you shall not use My name to make false promises, and so profane the name of your God; I am Adonai.

You shall not wrong your neighbor or cheat her. The wages of a hired servant shall not remain with you all night until the morning. You shall not insult the deaf nor trip the blind, but you shall be in awe of your God: I am Adonai.

You shall do no injustice in judgment; you shall not be partial to the poor nor favor the great, but in righteousness shall you judge your neighbor.

You shall not go up and down as a rumormonger among your people, and you shall not stand idly by the blood of your neighbor: I am Adonai.

¹⁷You shall not hate your sister in your heart, but you shall rebuke your neighbor, and not bear sin because of him. ¹⁸You shall not take vengeance nor bear a grudge against the members of your own people, **but you shall love your neighbor as yourself**: I am Adonai.

BUT YOU SHALL LOVE YOUR NEIGHBOR AS YOURSELF
(LEVITICUS 19.18)

I learned how to love another person by drinking in a bar. Two friends were drinking together. One asked the other, "Do you love me?" Ivan answered the question, "Of course." Then the first friend asked, "Do you know what gives me pain?" Ivan answered, "Not really." "Then you do not really love me." Loving people is knowing their pain. (Rabbi Moshe Leib of Sasov)

Do you know what causes your best friend's pain? Does he or she know about you?

Experiences

Do one of these things.

Rap the Holiness Code

List the rules in the Holiness Code. Then work in a group to turn them into a rap.

Make Your Own List of Things that Make You Holy

Work as a group and make a list of things you would consider to be part of your own Holiness Code. These should be things the doing of which makes you holy.

Have a K'doshim Kongress

Vote on the Holiness Code. Discuss and vote on every rule in the Holiness Code. Add ones that you think are missing.

THE SPIES (NUMBERS 13:17–14:23)

Here we are in the middle of the book of Numbers. We are still in the first year in the wilderness. We have neared the Land of Canaan and now are ready to spy out the land.

SENDING SPIES

Narrator 1: ¹³ʸMoses sent men to spy out the land of Canaan, and said to them:

Moses: Go up to the Negev and go up into the hill country, ¹⁸and see what the land is, and whether the people who live in it are strong or weak, whether they are few or many, ¹⁹and whether the land that they live in is good or bad, and whether the cities that they live in are like camps or forts, ²⁰and whether the land is rich or poor, and whether there is wood in it or not. Be brave and bring some of the fruit of the land.

Narrator 2: Now the time was the season of the first ripe grapes. So they went up and spied out the land... And they came to the Valley of Eshcol and cut down from there a branch with a single cluster of grapes, and they carried it on a pole between two of them; they brought also some pomegranates and figs.

Narrator 1: At the end of forty days they returned from spying out the land, and they came to Moses and Aaron and to all the congregation of the Families-of-Israel in the wilderness of Paran, at Kadesh; they brought back word to them and to all the community and showed them the fruit of the land. They told them:

THE REPORT

The Spies: **We came to the land to which you sent us; it flows with milk and honey, and this is its fruit. Yet the people who dwell in the land are strong, and the cities are forts and very large...** The Amalekites dwell in the land of the Negev; the Hittites, the Jebusites, and the Amorites dwell in the hill country; and the Canaanites dwell by the sea and along the Jordan.

Narrator 2: But Caleb quieted the people facing Moses, and said:

Caleb: Let us go up at once and occupy it; for we are well able to overcome it.

Narrator 1: Then the men who had gone up with him said,

The Spies: We are not able to go up against the people, for they are stronger than we.

Narrator 1: So they brought to the people of Israel an evil report of the land that they had spied out, saying:

The Spies: The land through which we have gone, to spy it out, is a land that eats its inhabitants; and all the people that we saw are giants... and we seemed to ourselves like grasshoppers, and so we seemed to them.

THE COMPLAINTS

Narrator 1: Then all of the community raised a loud shout; and the people wept that night. And all the Families-of-Israel whispered against Moses and Aaron; the whole community said to them:

Families-of-Israel: It would have been better to have died in the land of Egypt! Or would that we had died in this wilderness! Why does Adonai bring us into this land, to die by the sword? Our wives and our little ones will become victims. It would be better for us to go back to Egypt.

Narrator 1: And they said to one another:

Families-of-Israel: Let us choose a leader and go back to Egypt.

Narrator 2: Then Moses and Aaron fell on their faces before all the gathered community of the Families-of-Israel. And Joshua, the son of Nun, and Caleb, the son of Jephunneh, who were among those who had spied out the land, tore their clothes and said to all the community of the Families-of-Israel,

Joshua & Caleb:	The land that we passed through to spy it out is a wonderfully good land. If Adonai delights in us, God will bring us into this land and give it to us, a land which flows with milk and honey. Only do not rebel against Adonai; and do not fear the people of the land, for... Adonai is with us; do not fear them.

GOD'S LAMENT

Narrator 2:	But all the congregation said to stone them with stones. Then Adonai appeared at the tent of meeting to all the Families-of-Israel. And Adonai said to Moses:
God:	How long will this people despise Me? And how long will they not believe in Me, even after all the signs that I have done for them? I will strike them with disease and disinherit them, and I will make of you a nation greater and mightier than they.

MOSES TALKS GOD DOWN

Narrator 1:	But Moses said Adonai,
Moses:	If you do that, the Egyptians will hear of it, for You brought this people up with Your might from among them...

Now if You do kill this people, then the nations who have heard Your fame will say, Because Adonai was not able to bring this people into the land that God swore to give to them, God instead has slain them in the wilderness."

I pray You, let the power of Adonai be great as You have promised, saying,

God: Adonai is slow to anger and endless in kindness, forgiving sins and mistakes...

Moses: **Pardon the sins of this people, I pray,** according to Your great kindness...

Narrator 2: Then Adonai said:

God: I have forgiven as you said; but I swear... none of the people who have seen My glory and My signs that I did in Egypt and in the wilderness, and (still)... have not listened to My voice, shall see the land that I swore to give to their ancestors; and none of those who hated Me shall see it.

PARDON THE SINS OF THIS PEOPLE, I PRAY (NUMBERS 14:19)

Moses reminds God that God pardoned Israel for the idolatry that they practiced in Egypt. Even though they had not remained faithful to the One God, God still took them out of Egypt. This time was not as bad as worshipping idols. You should do the same again and redeem them at this moment. (Moshe Lieb of Sasov)

When have you needed to be forgiven?

Experiences

Do one of these things.

Make a Spy Video

Shoot a spy's POV (point of view) video. Show the land of Israel the way that the spies saw it. If you want, shoot an alternative video from Joshua and Caleb's POV.

Do a Paper-Tear Midrash

Do a paper-tear midrash of the land of Israel and all the things that the spies saw.

Moses to Aaron and Miriam

Create a conversation between Moses, Miriam and Aaron. You can write or perform this conversation. It should take place after this story. It should reveal all their feelings about the spies, the people's choice, God's anger, and God's penalty.

Debate Entering the Land

Some Jews (ten spies) wanted to abandon the land of Israel. Some Jews (two spies) wanted to go ahead and conquer the land of Israel. Stage the debate.

MAH TOVU (NUMBERS 22:1–36, 24:2–5)

We have skipped a little bit of the book of Numbers. We are now forty years into the time in the Wilderness. The Families-of-Israel are moving into position to enter the land of Israel.

THE FIRST BRIBE

Narrator 1: ²²The Families-of-Israel set out and camped in the plains of Moab—beyond the Jordan—at Jericho. ²And Balak, the son of Zippor, saw all that Israel had done to the Amorites. ³And Moab was in great fear of the people, because they were many; Moab was overcome with fear of the Families-of-Israel. ⁴And Moab said to the elders of Midian:

Moab: This horde will now take over all that is around us…

Narrator 2: So Balak the son of Zippor, who was king of Moab at that time, sent messengers to Bilaam saying:

Balak: Behold, a people has come out of Egypt; they cover the face of the earth, and they are dwelling opposite me. Please curse this people for me, since they are too mighty for me; perhaps I shall be able to defeat them and drive them from the land; for I know that he whom you bless is blessed, and he whom you curse is cursed.

Narrator 1: So the elders of Moab and the elders of Midian departed with the fees for sorcery in their hand; and they came to Bilaam and gave him Balak's message. And Bilaam said to them:

Bilaam: Sleep here tonight, and I will bring back word to you, what Adonai tells to me.

Narrator 2: So the princes of Moab stayed with Bilaam. And God came to Bilaam and said:

God: Who are these men with you?

Narrator 2: And Bilaam said to God:

Bilaam: Balak, the son of Zippor, king of Moab, has sent them to me, saying, "Here, a people has come out of Egypt, and it covers the face of the earth. Now, come, curse them for me; perhaps I shall be able to fight against them and drive them out."

Narrator 1: God said to Bilaam:

God: You shall not go with them; you shall not curse the people, for they are blessed.

Narrator 2: Bilaam rose in the morning and said to the princes of Balak:

Bilaam: Go to your own land, for Adonai has refused to let me go with you.

Narrator 1: So the princes of Moab got up and went to Balak, and said:

Elders: Bilaam refuses to come with us.

THE SECOND BRIBE

Narrator 2: Once again Balak sent princes. They were more in number and more honorable than before. They came to Bilaam and said to him:

Princes: Balak the son of Zippor says: "Let nothing keep you from coming to me; for I will definitely do you great honor, and whatever you say to me I will do; come, curse this people for me."

Narrator 1: But Bilaam answered and said to the servants of Balak:

Bilaam: Even if Balak were to give me his house full of silver and gold, I could not go beyond the command of Adonai, my God, to do less or more. Please stay here tonight so that I may know what more Adonai will say to me.

Narrator 2: God came to Bilaam at night and said to him:

God: Since the men have come to call you, get up, go with them; but do only what I tell you to do.

BILAAM TRAVELS

Narrator 1: Bilaam rose in the morning and saddled his donkey and went with the princes of Moab. But God got angry because he went. The angel of Adonai stood in his way to oppose him. Now he was riding on the donkey, and his two servants were with him.

Narrator 2: And the donkey saw the angel of Adonai standing in the road with a drawn sword in his hand; and the donkey turned out of the road and went into the field. Bilaam struck the donkey, to turn her into the road. Then the angel of Adonai stood in a narrow path between the vineyards, with a wall on either side. When the donkey saw the angel of Adonai she pushed against the wall and pressed Bilaam's foot against the wall; so he struck her again.

THEN ADONAI OPENED THE MOUTH OF THE DONKEY

(NUMBERS 22:28)

Balak knew that Moses was a famous orator. He hired Bilaam to defeat him, because Bilaam was famous. He thought Israel's power was in Moses' words. He was wrong. To show him that, God turned a donkey into a great orator, too. (Imrei Kohen)

Does God have a sense of humor?

Narrator 1: Then the angel of Adonai went ahead and stood in a narrow place, where there was no way to turn either to the right or to the left. When the donkey saw the angel of Adonai she lay down under Bilaam; and Bilaam's anger was kindled, and he struck the donkey with his staff. **Then Adonai opened the mouth of the donkey, and she said to Bilaam:**

Donkey: What did I do to you that you have hit me three times?

Narrator 2: And Bilaam said to the donkey:

Bilaam: Because you have made fun of me. I wish I had a sword in my hand, for then I would kill you.

Narrator 1: And the donkey said to Bilaam:

Donkey: Am I not your donkey, on which you have ridden all your life to this day? Have I ever done THIS to you before?

Narrator 2: And he said:

Bilaam: No.

Narrator 1: Then Adonai opened Bilaam's eyes, and he saw the angel of Adonai standing in the way with his drawn sword in his hand. Bilaam bowed his head and fell on his face. And the angel of Adonai said to him:

Angel: Why have you hit your donkey three times? Here, I have come forward to stop you, because you are doing the wrong thing before me; and the donkey saw me, and turned aside before me these three times. If she had not turned aside from me, right now I would have killed you and let her live.

Narrator 2: ³Then Bilaam said to the angel of Adonai:

Bilaam: I have sinned. I did not know that you stood in the road to stop me. Now if it is evil in your sight, I will go back.

Narrator 1: ³The angel of Adonai said to Bilaam:

Angel: Go with the men; but only say the words that I tell you to say.

Narrator 2: So Bilaam went on with the princes of Balak. ³⁶When Balak heard that Bilaam had come, he went out to meet him at the city of Moab, on the boundary formed by the Arnon, at the edge of the border…²⁴¹And Bilaam lifted up his eyes and saw Israel encamping tribe by tribe. And the Spirit of God came upon him, ³and he took up his speech, and said:

BILAAM'S CURSE BECOMES A BLESSING

Bilaam: The speaking of Bilaam the son of Beor, the speaking of the man whose eyes are opened, ⁴the speaking of him who hears the words of God, who sees the vision of the High One, falling down, but having his eyes uncovered:

³How good are your tents, Jacob, your encampments, Israel!

HOW GOOD ARE YOUR TENTS, JACOB, YOUR ENCAMPMENTS, ISRAEL! (NUMBERS 24:5)

Tents are the way you look. This is their connection to Jacob. Encampments are what's inside. This is their connection to Israel. (Ba'al Shem Tov)

What are some of the differences between your outside and your inside?

Experiences

Do one of these things.

Interviews

Imagine you are a reporter.

- Ask Bilaam, "Why does God listen to you?"
- Ask Balak, "Why did you want Bilaam to curse Israel? Why not just fight them?"
- Ask God, "Why did you let Bilaam go to Balak and try to curse?"
- Ask the donkey, "Why did you wait so long to start talking?"

Make a Model of the Israelite Camp

There is a midrash that what made Israel's tents appear "goodly" was the fact that they were set up so that no tent looked into another tent. Design the Israelite camp. Put the Tabernacle in the center. You've got some research to do before you start to build.

ALMOST THE PROMISED LAND (DEUTERONOMY 34:1-12)

We are finally at the end of the book of Deuteronomy. The time in the wilderness is over, and Israel is just about to cross over into the land. At the end of the Torah, Moses dies.

Narrator 1: [34:1]Moses went up from the plains of Moab to Mount Nebo, on top of the Pisgah (which is across from Jericho). Adonai showed him all the land of Israel. From Gilead to Dan, [2]all of Naphtali, the land of Ephraim and Manasseh. From all the land of Judah to the Mediterranean Sea. The Negev. From the Plain of Jericho to Zoar. Adonai said to him:

God: This is the land which I promised to Abraham, to Isaac, and to Jacob, saying: "To your future-family I will give it." I let you see it with your own eyes, but you will not cross into it.

Narrator 2: **Moses, Adonai's servant, died there, in the land of Moab, by the word of Adonai.** Adonai buried him in the valley of the land of Moab, and no person knows his grave to this day.

Narrator 1: Moses was 120 years old when he died. His eyes were still bright, and he was still strong.

Narrator 2: The children of Israel wept for Moses for thirty days. The days of weeping for Moses ended. Joshua, son of Nun, was filled with the spirit of wisdom because Moses had touched him. The Families-of-Israel listened to him.

Narrator 1: Never again will Israel have a prophet like Moses, who knew Adonai face to face. for all the signs and wonders that God sent him to do in the land of Egypt, to Pharaoh and all his workers and all his land, and for the mighty hand and wonders, that Moses made happen before the eyes of all Israel.

Experiences

Do one of these things.

Moses' Ethical Will

An ethical will is the wisdom a person wants to leave for those who come after her/him. The whole book of Deuteronomy is a kind of ethical will for Moses. Look through the book of Deuteronomy and write a short ethical will for Moses.

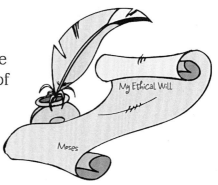

A Eulogy for Moses

No one knows where Moses is buried, but that shouldn't stop you from having a memorial service. Write a eulogy for Moses. Tell everyone what Moses meant to you.

Video Joshua's First Press Conference

Joshua takes over from Moses. Video Joshua's first press conference. What are the things that the Families-of-Israel want to know? What are the answers that Joshua wants to give? Include thoughts of entering the land of Israel.